Needlework
—School—

*A modern piece of three-dimensional quilting
called 'One foot Square.*

Needlework
School

*A comprehensive guide to decorative embroidery by
The Embroiderers' Guild Practical Study Group.*

NEW
BURLINGTON
BOOKS

A QUARTO BOOK

Published by New Burlington Books
6 Blundell Street
London N7 9BH

Copyright © 1982 Quarto Publishing Limited

Reprinted 1987

ISBN 1 85348 030 4

Art Editor Hilary Krag
Art Director Alastair Campbell
Editors Dorothea Hall, Jim Miles
Editorial Director Christopher Fagg
Paste-up Artists Penny Dawes, Debbie Riviere, Gerry Sandford
Photographer Jon Wyand
Artist Terry Evans
The publishers wish to express their gratitude for major contributions by
the following people:

Authors
Muriel Best, Vicky Lugg, Dorothy Tucker

Contributors
Jenny Blackburn, Sylvia Bramley, Jenny Bullen, Christine Cooper,
Jeanette Durrant, Jane Lemon, Sheila Miller, Jean Mould, Daphne
Nicholson, Maureen Pallister, Herta Puls, Margaret Rivers, Dorothy Sim,
Marjorie Williams, Mary Youles

Filmset in Great Britain QV Typesetting Ltd, London
Colour origination in Hong Kong by Hong Kong Graphic Arts
Printed in Hong Kong by Leefung-Asco Printers Limited

CONTENTS

FOREWORD

LEFT: *This is a fragment of sixth century Coptic tapestry weaving from Egypt woven in wool on a linen ground.*

BELOW: *In contrast, this contemporary example is of multi-coloured strips of silk interwoven through paper fragments, some of which are painted. Lines of red and white machine stitching are added to the surface.*

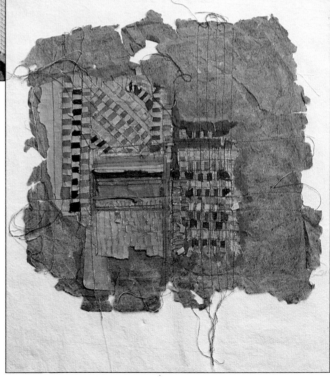

I think it an excellent idea that the authors of this book — all of whom I have known for years — should have worked together to produce such a comprehensive amount of information in one volume.

The contributors are all members of the Practical Study Group of the Embroiderers' Guild of Great Britain, which was inaugurated in 1973. As embroiderers they hope to extend their knowledge to others by teaching groups of people eager to study the craft. They have all trained as painters, graphic designers or textile artists and have come to regard embroidery as their main interest. Each one of the authors has a quite different approach to her particular area, whether it is drawing, lettering or clothing decoration. They all teach embroidery courses in different parts of the United Kingdom on a part-time basis and regularly exhibit their own work. Through the years they have acquired a thorough knowledge of the craft through practical work and experimentation; the result is expertise of an extremely high standard on design techniques, materials and threads. This book is based on the experience of what they have found to be useful to beginners and advanced embroiderers alike.

The various sections cover all the major techniques of a subject that comprise a vast range of work. I find the format of the book very useful with both text and illustrations integrating in a visually stimulating and helpful way. I particularly like the inclusion of historical examples of embroidery with modern counterparts: an invitation to the serious embroiderer to delve into the craft's fascinating past.

Colour — so often lacking in books on technique — is here in delightful profusion. I consider colour next to design in importance because it can be so expressive when using stitches and fabrics to convey mood and depth — it affects us in surprising ways. The section on the altering of the surface of a fabric could lead to fascinating experiments, and the same is true of the sections on changing the scale of stitches and the use of different weights of thread. The points on framing are important as a lack of these basic considerations often ruins good work.

Altogether I feel that the authors and publishers have done a marvellous job with a book that can be perused again and again, with new ideas surfacing each time. It has been written from first-hand experience and, having seen it, I immediately want to start a new piece of work.

Constance Howard

INTRODUCTION
HOW TO USE THIS BOOK

Needlework School offers a structured course in embroidery and, although designed to develop section by section, each chapter is complete in itself.

The first part of the book deals with basic information on equipment, stitches, fabrics, design and colour; the second part introduces techniques. Basic instructions are given for the principal methods used in embroidery today, together with brief histories, ending with information on fastenings and finishings. The third and final part of the book contains design developments, each one utilizing a different approach and source of inspiration. A practical hints chapter explaining ways of mounting and framing concludes the course, together with a book list for further reading on specialist subjects, and a guide to Museums and Galleries.

Although for most people embroidery is regarded as a hobby, there are those who wish to take it further by gaining some form of qualification in the subject; for these people the book will provide an excellent introduction to an examination syllabus.

Throughout the book developments or exercises have been suggested. It is worth keeping a portfolio for filing samples for reference — a loose-leaf file with plastic sleeves is a good idea, not only for worked examples but also for any drawings and photographs that might be useful for future projects. It is always helpful, particularly as a source of reference, to collect and enter your ideas and developments in the order in which they were made. In this way, you will be able to see clearly the progression of your original idea.

When a certain measure of confidence in design and technique is achieved a more experimental approach can be taken, and then some of the rules can be broken, but remember not to have too many conflicting ideas and techniques in any one project. The simplest design is usually the most effective.

It is intended that this book should be a useful source of reference and inspiration so that, through practice, techniques and ideas can combine to provide the stimulus for developing your own skills and creative approaches. For example a development idea from the earlier part of the book could be explored after learning a technique outlined later on such as cutwork.

The paragraphs below outline the main points and aims of all parts of the book.

Designing with stitches

In this section creative stitching is emphasized. It explains how stitches are used to express movement, direction, tonal values and line, and how they can create varying textures. Many basic stitches are illustrated in step by step diagrams and can be used as a foundation for creative stitching.

Looking at fabrics

The structure of the different fabrics used in embroidery is clearly defined and individual qualities outlined. In this chapter it is suggested that by collecting and handling as many different types of fabric as possible, the embroiderer will have a greater awareness of his or her individual potential. Techniques for dyeing and space-dyeing are fully explored.

Designing

The reader is introduced in this chapter to many ways of selecting and translating original ideas into embroidery. Sources of inspiration are suggested such as looking at lines in rock strata, and interiors in different lights of the day. This is followed by sections about designing from photographs, working with colour, understanding tonal values, mood and movement. New concepts of contemporary design and methods of display are also thoroughly explored.

Stitching on evenweave

Embroidery on evenweave fabric is given the overall name of counted thread. The simple regular weave of the background fabric influences the characteristics of methods used. This is embellished in a number of ways by a variety of stitches and techniques to give richly patterned effects. Much of the work relies on the subtleties of monochrome, and others exploit the colours of the spectrum.

Altering the surface

The surface of the fabric is fully explored and exploited in this chapter: it can be cut to create decorative holes, as in cutwork; it can be manipulated by pleating, gathering, folding and smocking, which will create shadows and a three-dimensional effect. The surface can be raised by the addition of wadding with the layers held in place by stitching giving a pleasing padded effect. Techniques covered include English, Italian and trapunto quilting. Stitches can also be worked over shapes made by padding with felt or by adding free standing motifs, as described in stumpwork, where the embroidery has the appearance of a low-relief carving.

Appliqué

Appliqué involves stitching layers of different fabrics together in a variety of decorative ways. Each technique is fully explored and is accompanied by clear diagrams and instructions. These include broderie perse, inlay — using several layers of coloured fabrics, as seen in South American mola work, Hawaiian appliqué, appliqué from the Meo hilltribes of Thailand, traditional appliqué using both hand and machine stitching.

Patchwork

Patchwork has developed greatly since it was first used as an economical way of recycling fabric oddments and has become a very sophisticated craft. The technique in essence relies on the use of coloured fabrics to create patterned surfaces. The varieties of patchwork demonstrated in the section include handsewn, strip, crazy, Seminole, shell, Suffolk puff, cathedral window, folded star, log cabin, random and pieced-block.

Whitework

Embroidery on white fabric embraces some of the most intricate and oldest forms of embroidery. In the chapter, the techniques are divided into two groups: the first covers embroidery on fine, sheer fabrics such as Ayrshire, Carrickmacross and Indian chikan work. The second group covers embroidery on opaque fabrics such as surface embroidery, cutwork, Hardanger, Hedebo, Mountmellick, needlepoint and broderie anglaise.

Metal thread

Metal thread is the richest type of embroidery and can involve special techniques for applying pure gold and silver threads, precious jewels and gem stones to ground fabrics of the highest quality. Through history, this embroidery has maintained an exceptionally high standard of design and craftsmanship, and was usually worked by professional designers and embroiderers. Techniques illustrated in the chapter include laid work, simple couching, underside couching, basketwork, couching in lines and spirals, applying sequins, beads and mica.

Machine embroidery

The full potential of machine embroidery is explored. Traditional techniques are adapted for machining appliqué, braid and decorative stitch patterns, plus some unusual textural effects. In contrast to this, the following section explores free machine embroidery where the machine needle is used, as an artist might use a pencil, to draw, scribble or doodle ideas directly onto a ground fabric. The sewing threads can be tightened or loosened allowing the stitching to fill areas on the surface of the fabric. Freely interpreted designs, landscapes and figurative compositions are developed.

Fastenings and finishings

In this section, different ways of fastening and finishing are suggested that would give the finishing touch to a selected piece of work. Techniques cover making frog fasteners, Turk's head knots, cords and braids, buttons, decorative seams and edges, facings and bindings, fringes and tassels. All of these may be elaborated upon or used as a focal point to suit an individual style.

Themes and developments

In this section, which covers painted textiles, marbling on fabric and felt and paper making, individual embroiderers have taken a theme and developed it in their own particular way. Some have been concerned with the preparation of the background surface, using paints and dyes while others have made constructions of paper and felt and used these as a starting point for their creative embroidery. The techniques used include stencilling, spraying, airbrushing, crayoning, and stitching on paper. Other projects are based on designs from nature — flowers and animals, and manmade objects such as paint boxes, staircases and letters. The embroidery is approached in an exploratory way so that the section is design- rather than technique-based.

Practical hints

In this section original and creative ways of framing and mounting embroidery are discussed. They include making traditional mounts and frames, free-hanging surrounds, fabric-covered — as separate frames and frames integral to the embroidery. Clear instructions are given for enlarging designs, turning corners, dressing a frame, damp-stretching embroidery, mounting and lacing, and picture framing.

◆

BASIC EQUIPMENT

Embroidery materials

It is not necessary to have an extensive collection of sewing equipment. Decide which items are most important, and build on these basics over time. It is too easy to be seduced by dazzling displays of threads.

Fabrics and threads can be bought from department stores and specialist shops throughout the country. Some shops and small firms run mail order services; their addresses can be found in embroidery magazines.

The basic tools are quite simple. You need a selection of needles for different uses; pins; a bodkin; a thimble; a stiletto; tape measure and tacking cotton. Apart from dressmaking shears, fine embroidery scissors with sharp points, are essential. Beeswax is necessary for metal thread work. An embroidery frame will help with some techniques; it is essential when using metal threads.

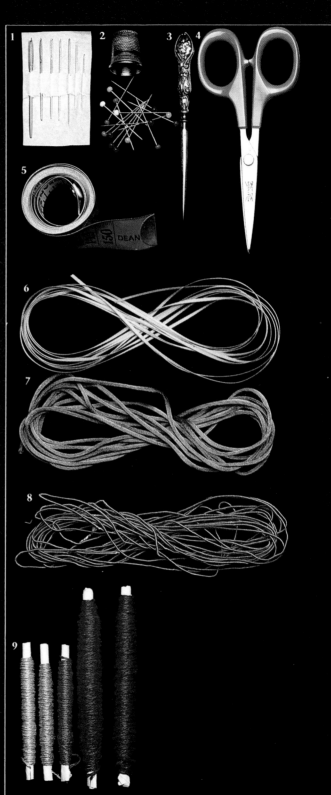

BELOW: *Frames are required for some kinds of work. The large stand (back) leaves both hands free, but the work must be laced into position. Tacks can be used on the square frame without a stand (middle). The small round frames (front) are used for fine work. The small palette (front left) is used to keep lengths of thread tidy.*

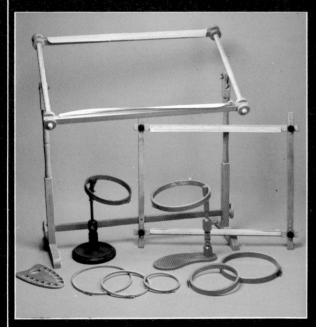

RIGHT: **1** *Selection of needles, including a bodkin, tapestry, crewel, sewing and beading,* **2** *Thimble and glass-beaded pins,* **3** *Stiletto,* **4** *Embroidery scissors,* **5** *Tape measure,* **6** *Narrow ribbon,* **7** *Rat tail cord,* **8** *Bourdon cord,* **9** *Linen threads,* **10** *Flower threads,* **11, 12, 13** *Coton perlé,* **14, 15** *Stranded cottons (shaded),* **16, 17** *Cordonnet,* **18, 19, 20** *Machine thread,* **21, 22, 23** *Coton à broder,* **24, 25** *Stranded cottons,* **26** *Crewel wool,* **27** *Persian wool,* **28, 29** *Tapestry wool,* **30** *Bouclé* **31** *Knitting yarn.*

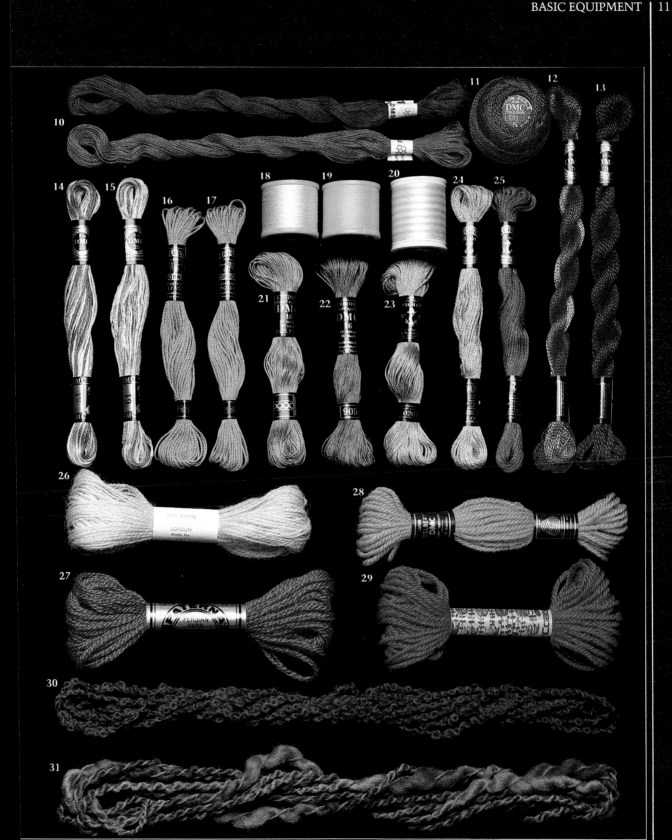

1 Setsquare, 2 Notebook,
3 Compasses, 4 Drawing
pins, 5 Plastic eraser,
6 Pencil sharpener,
7 Fixative, 8 Spray diffuser,
9 Shears, 10 Craft knife,
11 Steel rule, 12 Felt-tip
markers, 13 Technical pens,
14 Non-clogging ink,
15 Cartridge paper,
16 Squared paper, 17 Tracing
paper, 18 Sketch book,
19 Brushes, 20 Watercolours,
21 Gouaches, 22 Conté
crayons, 23 Charcoal,
24 Chalks, 25 Pencils. Many
items can be bought at any
good art shop, but it would
not be essential to buy them
all at first.

Design materials

The range of design tools available is enormous. Each tool has a specific function; consider them in the light of your own needs, and choose with care.

There is no need to spend a great deal of money, but in the long run, it is worth buying the best you can afford.

Accuracy is important in any design that is to be directly transferred. Secure your paper to a drawing board with drawing pins or clips. Invest in a good large setsquare, for true right angles. Compasses have an obvious use in drawing circles, but they can also be used for constructing and bisecting angles, and, with an extra point, converted into dividers for measuring small equal spaces.

Cleanliness is a factor when using charcoal or pencil drawings near delicate silks. A good-quality plastic eraser is less messy than a cheap rubber one. Always use fixative on your designs; as well as preserving them, it stops dirty smudges on hands or work. It can be applied with a spray diffuser, or bought in aerosol form.

A good pair of shears is essential; for cutting straight lines on paper or board use a craft knife with a metal rule. Both have many other uses.

Paper is available in a huge variety of weights, colours and textures. A basic minimum is sheets of cartridge for drawing and painting; tracing paper and squared paper, for ready measurement, and for scaling work up and down to size. Record materials used and decisions taken in a notebook, and never go anywhere without your sketch-book, to record things seen and visual ideas. Attach swatches of coloured paper or fabric, when possible.

The range of drawing, colouring and painting materials is almost endless. Get a variety of materials which make different kinds of marks, rather than spend all your money on dozens of different colours in the same medium. Drawing equipment can range in use from the freedom of charcoal drawing to the precision of the technical pen. Felt-tip markers, for fast free work in colour, are cheap and readily available. Technical pens are expensive, but they give a fine clean line. Non-clogging ink is essential. Conté crayons, charcoal and chalk are good for free sketching. Pencils, in a range of hardnesses, are indispensible.

The basic paints are watercolour and gouache. Watercolour is transparent, gouache opaque. A small pocket box of watercolours will do to start; gouaches can be bought in tubes as needed. Lamp black, zinc white, cadmium red (pale), cadmium yellow (pale), yellow ochre and cobalt blue would provide a basic palette. Choose brushes carefully, and take care of them in use. Three will be enough: sizes 1 (small), 4 (medium), and 7 or 8 (large). Sable is best, but expensive; however, with care, sable brushes will last for years.

DESIGNING WITH STITCHES

Throughout the past centuries the use of stitches has been influenced by the fashion of the day, and the availability of fabrics and threads. Embroiderers often copied designs and patterns from books of designs printed especially for craftsmen and women, or drawn out by professional designers who toured the country. Fortunately, embroiderers today are released from these inhibitions, and the number of ways of creating a personal design is infinite.

Translating a design into stitches

When selecting stitches to work your design, do not forget that the same stitch can be varied according to the thickness of the thread used and the size, direction, and density in which the stitches are worked. The choice of threads will considerably affect the appearance of the stitches used. Limit the colour scheme to two or three colours, or tones of one colour; the accent should be on the stitches. Overlap stitches to create a rich texture; herringbone, cretan and wave worked in this way will give the effect of wire mesh, while French knots and bullion knots piled closely together will produce a knubbly texture which looks effective if matt and shiny threads are mixed. Interesting patterns can be built up by couching thick threads with fine ones using a different stitch for each couched thread.

Cretan stitch is a looped stitch which can be worked either close together to shape leaves for example, or open to form a straight border. Working from left to right, bring the needle out on the bottom line. Make a short vertical stitch downwards from the top line a short distance away (**1**). Make a similar stitch upwards from the bottom line (**2**). Continue in this way to complete row (**3**).

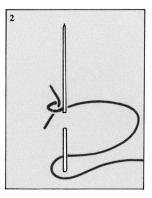

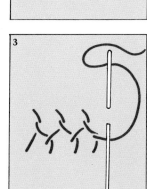

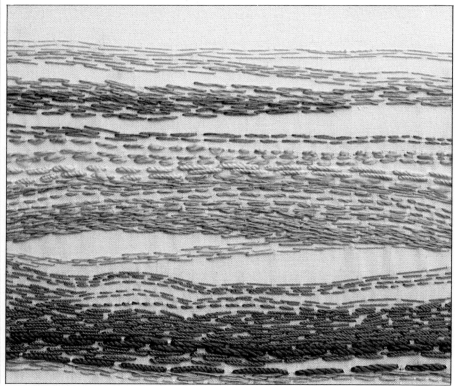

LEFT: *Rows of running stitch, using different thicknesses of twisted silk in tones of one colour, are used to build up a design. The stitches range in size from very small ones in fine thread, to larger ones in thicker thread. In places, the stitches are worked in close rows to give density and weight, in contrast with the more openly stitched areas. Simple landscape designs can be built up in this way, using variations of one stitch.*

Wave stitch is a lacy filling stitch. Begin by working a row of small evenly spaced upright stitches (**1**). Bring needle out on line below, a little to right, pass it behind stitch above and insert it to left in a direct line between upright stitches above (**2**). Continue working to row end (**3**). Repeat working in opposite direction (**4**) passing needle behind threads of previous row (**5**). Repeat on following rows (**6**).

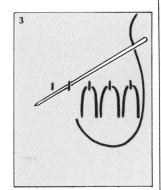

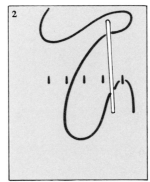

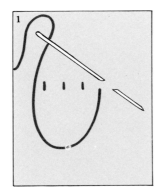

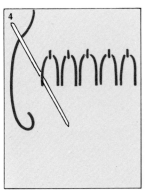

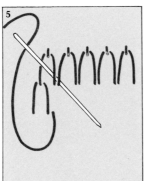

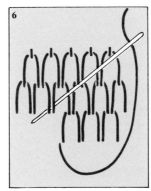

BELOW: *In this view of a landscape, areas of densely-worked French knots contrast with smoother areas of overlapping cretan and straight stitches. The piece is worked entirely in medium silk twist; the rich texture of stitches is complemented by the areas of smooth unworked background fabric.*

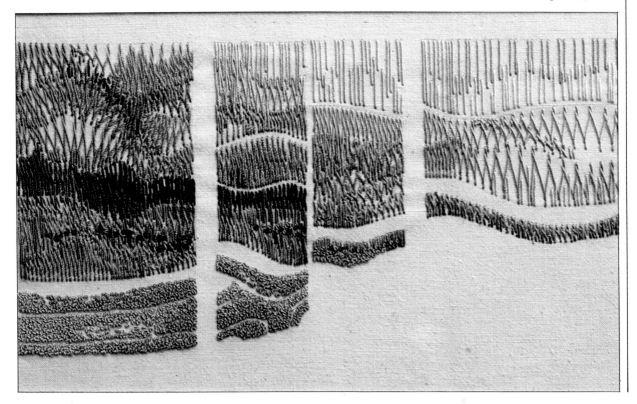

French knots can be worked separately or close together. Bring needle out, and holding thread firmly with left hand, twist needle twice around thread (**1**). Tighten the twisted thread (**2**) and insert needle close to starting point (**3**). Pull needle through to back of fabric leaving a well-shaped knot on the surface. Repeat as needed (**4**).

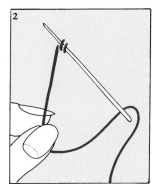

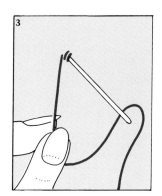

Bullion knots can be used as a filling or line stitch. Bring needle out, insert it a short distance away (the length of the bullion knot), and pull through needle point only. Twist thread around point five or six times (**1**). Carefully pull needle through without disturbing the twists (**2**). Pull working thread and coils tight (**3**) and reinsert needle at same point to keep knot flat (**4**).

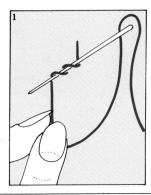

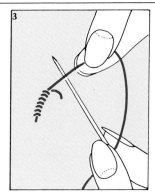

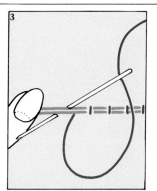

Couching: use for outlining or infilling. Bring out thread to be couched at right (**1**). Hold down to left. Bring out couching thread below. Make small upright stitch over laid threads and bring needle out below, a little to left (**2**). Continue to work evenly spaced stitches (**3**). Turn threads at row end and couch with horizontal stitch (**4**). Turn work around. Place stitches between those of previous row (**5**).

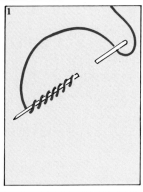

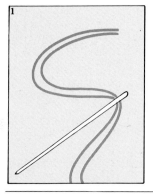

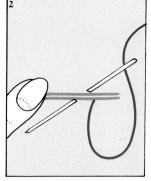

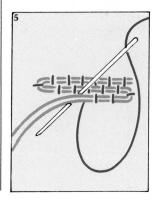

Variations of couching can be made either by working straight or slanting stitches spaced in regular groups (**1**), or by working different embroidery stitches over the threads, such as spaced buttonhole stitch (**2**), or open chain stitch (**3**). Increase the number of threads to be couched for a broader line.

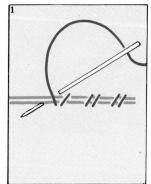

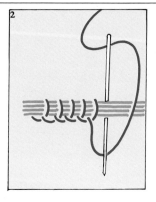

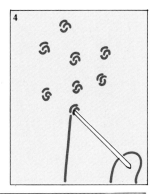

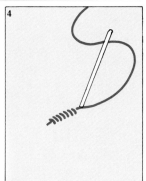

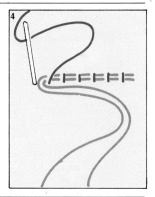

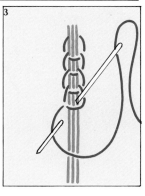

BELOW: *Overlapping lines of fly stitch worked in different weights of thread create a pattern of plant growth in this piece. The spiky lines of the stitch contrast with the roundness of the loosely worked French knots; they are echoed by the cretan and straight stitches.*

Create the feeling of free movement with stitches by varying their angle and direction. Tonal effects can be obtained by massing knots, or seeding them together and gradually thinning them out. Fly stitch is especially versatile; it can be worked with long, condensed lines of thread, or in short stitches. By turning the stitches to face each other or by working them in rows, a network can be made to fill an area.

Fly stitch is a looped stitch which can be worked either at random or in regular patterns. Bring needle out at left, and holding thread downwards, insert needle to right. Make a diagonal stitch to the centre and pull through (**1**). Hold the loop down with a short straight stitch (**2**). Work a repeat pattern in rows across (**3**).

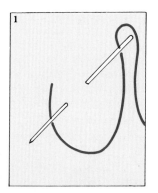

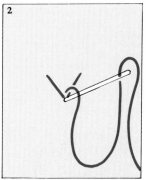

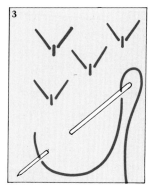

ABOVE: *This detail is taken from a set of colourful bed hangings embroidered in the late seventeenth century by Abigail Pett. The hangings are worked in crewel wool and show a wide variety of animals and plants. Stitches such as stem and long and short are used to fill solid areas contrasting with open patterned fillings. Great ingenuity is shown in this embroidery as no two areas are identical.*

STITCHES AS MARKS

Every stitch has particular qualities and can be used to create countless patterns and textures.

These examples are worked in coton à broder, fine cotton thread, perlé, soft cotton and crewel wool.

The left-hand column shows, from the top, seeding, fly stitch and detached chain stitch. The right-hand column shows blocks of straight stitch, circles of back stitch and French knots.

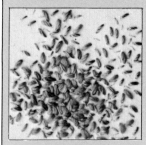

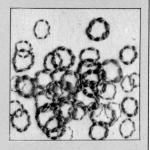

There are many ways of working a particular stitch, and the patterns and textures created can be used both formally and informally. Try working a stitch vertically, horizontally, or diagonally; upside-down; overlapping; in curves or spirals; in threads of contrasting thickness, or even in narrow strips of torn fabric.

Some stiches are more adaptable than others. Usually the simpler stitches are easier to exploit. Linear stitches, like cretan, stem and running, work well, as do isolated stitches like detached chain and fly.

Varying thicknesses of thread in tones of grey are used for this simple design. The change of direction of the stem stitch, and the choice of thread texture and weight make for a surface of subtle qualities. This contrasts with the rougher surface of French and bullion knots, showing some of the tactile possibilities of surface stitches.

Stem stitch is used mostly for lines and stems but it can also be worked in rows close together, as infilling. Bring needle out, make a short back stitch on line and bring out in middle with thread below needle point (**1**). Repeat along line, placing each stitch close together (**2**). For wide stem stitch insert needle at a slight angle, increasing angle for wider effect (**3**).

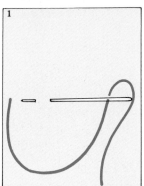

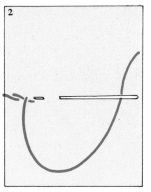

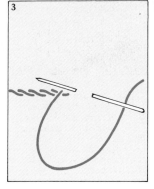

GROUPING STITCHES INTO FAMILIES

OUTLINE STITCHES

The main characteristic of this family of stitches is the linear quality, developing from the simplicity of running stitch to the raised and cord-line appearance of trailing Portuguese stem and scroll stitch. They are useful when stressing the linear aspect of a design. They can also be used closely packed to fill an area.

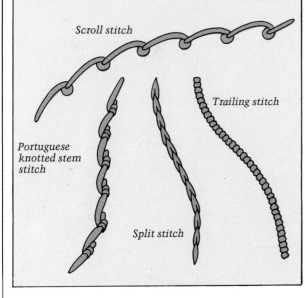

Scroll stitch

Trailing stitch

Portuguese knotted stem stitch

Split stitch

FLAT STITCHES

There is a wide range of stitches that are built up from the simple straight stitch. When repeated this can become satin, long and short or brick stitch, creating smooth areas of thread. The simple variations of cross stitch can develop into herringbone, leaf or chevron.

Long and short stitch

Leaf stitch

Fishbone stitch

LOOPED STITCHES

When working stitches from this group the method requires the thread to be looped under the needle to form the stitch. Simple buttonhole and blanket stitch are worked in rows, whereas fly stitch can be worked singly or in groups. Cretan stitch is particularly versatile.

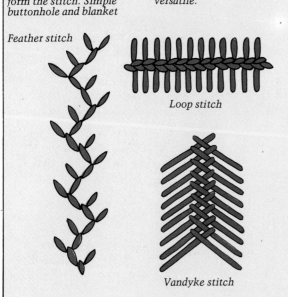

Feather stitch

Loop stitch

Vandyke stitch

CHAINED STITCHES

This is a comprehensive group of stitches and contains numerous variations. Most of them have a linear quality and the more complicated forms give a decorative raised line. Detached chain and wheatear stitch are worked separately. Simple chain is also used to give a solid filling.

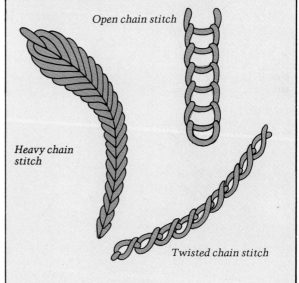

Open chain stitch

Heavy chain stitch

Twisted chain stitch

KNOTTED STITCHES

These form a useful group as they contrast with the flatter, smoother stitches. The single units of French knots and bullion knots can be worked closely together or scattered in a random manner. The knotted linear stitches like coral or knotted chain give a decorative effect.

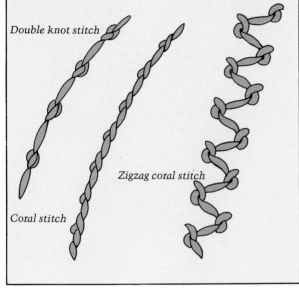

Double knot stitch

Zigzag coral stitch

Coral stitch

COUCHING STITCHES

Threads to be couched are laid on the surface of the material and held in place. A number of embroidery stitches like cross, detached chain or buttonhole can be used as well as the usual small straight stitch. Many of the decorative laid fillings are based on the couching technique.

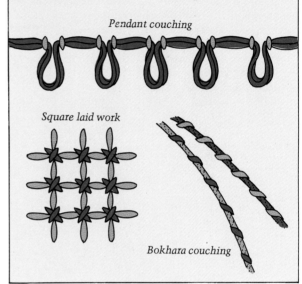

Pendant couching

Square laid work

Bokhara couching

FILLING STITCHES

A number of ways can be used to shade in an area of design. Individual stitches like seeding and sheaf give a speckled appearance, whereas cloud filling stitch makes a more regular effect. Couched laid threads give great variety and stitches like cretan and long and short are equally suitable.

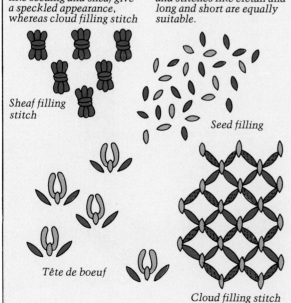

Sheaf filling stitch

Seed filling

Tête de boeuf

Cloud filling stitch

COMPOSITE STITCHES

The stitches in this group are worked in two or more stages. A foundation is worked on the fabric and onto this subsequent threads are looped or woven. Many basic stitches can be embellished in this way, including threaded back, chain and herringbone.

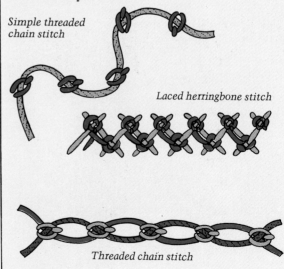

Simple threaded chain stitch

Laced herringbone stitch

Threaded chain stitch

BASIC STITCHES

Stitches are the embroiderer's alphabet; each one has its own characteristics. Practise working them in a medium weight smooth thread, such as perlé no. 5 or coton à broder, to learn the character of the stitch. Try each stitch in as wide a variety of threads as you can, noticing how the stitch is influenced by the thread that is used.

Choose a needle to suit the thread being used. The needle makes the hole in the fabric for the thread to slide through, so too large a one will leave an ugly gap; too fine a needle will be difficult to sew with and thread.

A medium weight calico, or soft cotton fabric is easy to work on. Put a piece of fabric on a frame, and try a variety of stitches and threads on one sampler.

Double running stitch is used mostly as an outline stitch in free-style embroidery. It is worked in two operations. Begin by working evenly spaced running stitches on the traced line. Then using the same coloured thread, work running stitches in the spaces left. Unlike back stitch, double running stitch is quite reversible.

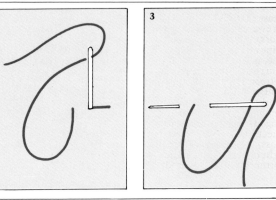

Back stitch is used extensively for outlining. Working from right to left, bring needle out on line, make a short straight stitch to right and bring needle out on line to left — the same distance from the starting point (1). Insert needle at starting point (2) and repeat along line working even stitches close together (3).

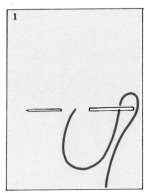  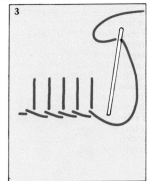

Blanket stitch, as its name implies, is used as an edging stitch but it can also be used for borders and outlining in both free-style and counted thread embroidery. Working from left to right, bring needle out on bottom line. Insert it on top line, to right, and bring out directly below with thread under needle (1). Repeat along row (2) and finish by inserting needle on bottom line (3).

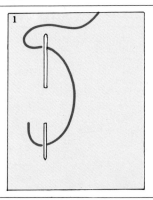 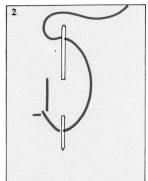 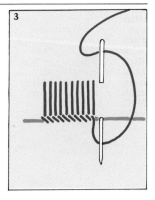

Buttonhole stitch is ordinarily used to give a firm edge to handmade button holes, but it is also used for cutwork and free-style motifs. It is worked like blanket stitch above but with the stitches placed close together (1). For a buttonhole stitch wheel, take the needle through the same central hole, spacing the outer stitches evenly (2). For a firm edge, work over a row of split stitch (3).

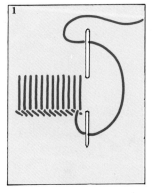 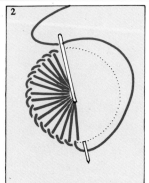

Chain stitch can be worked either as separate loops, outline or filling stitches. Bring needle out and make a straight stitch downwards inserting needle at starting point. Pull through with loop under needle point (**1**). Repeat, inserting needle where thread emerges (**2**). Finish row with a small stitch over last chain loop to secure (**3**).

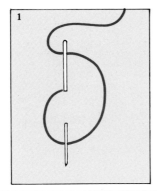 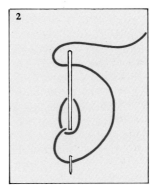 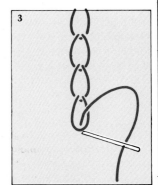

Cross stitch is best worked on evenweave fabric. Working from right to left, bring needle out on bottom line, take it to top left and bring out directly below on bottom line. Complete row of diagonal stitches (**1**). Working from left to right, complete crosses by making diagonal stitches in opposite direction (**2**). For a single cross, work from bottom right to top left, then from bottom left to top right (**3**).

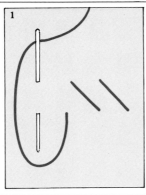 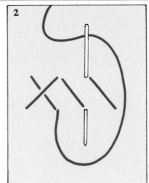 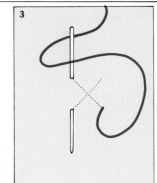

Herringbone stitch is used for lines and borders. Working from left to right, bring thread out, take it diagonally upwards and make a short back stitch on top line (**1**). Repeat making a similar stitch on bottom line, bringing needle out directly under starting point of stitch above (**2**). Continue in this way along row working evenly spaced stitches (**3**).

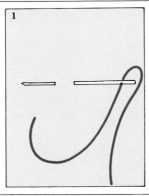 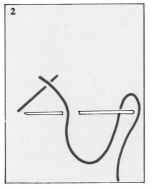 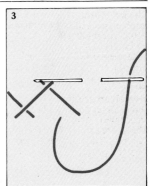

Satin stitch (upright) is used mostly as a line or border stitch. Begin on bottom line and make a short upright stitch (not longer than ¾ in (2cm). Bring needle out close to starting point (**1**). Make second stitch close to first (**2**). Complete the row, keeping an even tension (**3**).

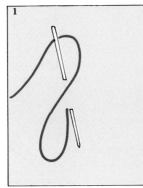 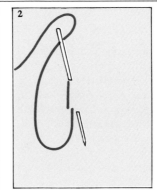 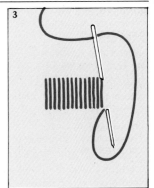

LOOKING AT FABRICS

The traditional fabrics which used to form the background for embroidery are continually being supplemented by new textiles to the extent that the selection can become overwhelming. The wrong choice of background fabric often leads to a disappointing piece of work, so selection with discrimination will save many hours of wasted effort. An understanding of the basic construction of different fabrics, together with handling samples of as many different fabrics as possible, will help considerably. The various techniques of embroidery relate closely to the qualities of the fabrics and threads used, and often to their availability in specific geographical areas. For example, the fine linens of northern Europe have formed the background for many of the lovely whitework and counted thread techniques. The rich endowment of natural fibres — wool, cotton, linen and silk — is now joined by the many synthetic yarns, all of which have their own specific qualities and characteristics.

Structure

Woven fabrics can range from a simple warp and weft to more complicated patterns such as herringbone, twill and damask. These strong patterns can be more difficult to use and in some instances it is hard at first to see whether the patterns are woven or embroidered. Embroidery on evenweave fabrics includes blackwork, canvaswork, cross-stitch, pulled work, pattern darning and drawn thread. The simple regular weave of the background fabric influences the characteristics of those methods.

Knitted fabrics are constructed with a continuous yarn, and are therefore more malleable and stretchy than woven structures.

Fabricated or non-woven fabrics are firm and do not fray. They range from the natural forms, leather, kid, and suede, to felt, vinyl and bonded interfacings. Other non-woven fabrics include both cotton and synthetic waddings.

Mesh fabrics have a twisted structure. They range from simple nets to the complicated lace patterns.

Texture

The texture of fabrics can vary enormously, depending on their constuction and density, and the type and weight of the yarn. Fabrics can be fine or coarse; smooth or rough; thin or thick; dull or lustrous; loosely or firmly woven, and endless combinations and variations of these characteristics exist. The construction yarn can be plyed, slubbed, woven to a complicated structure like bouclé or chenille and so on. The surface can also be affected by the finishing processes, such as napping and glazing, which are applied to textiles.

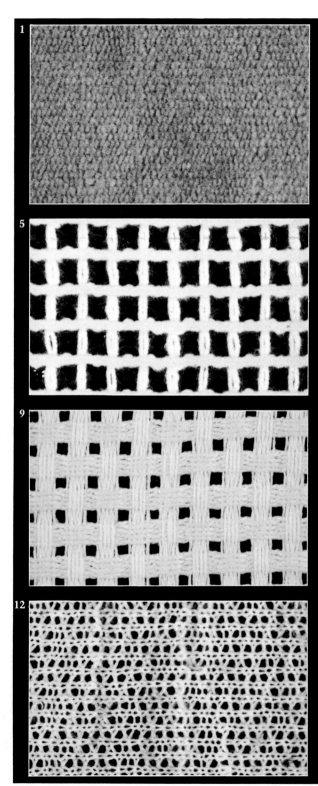

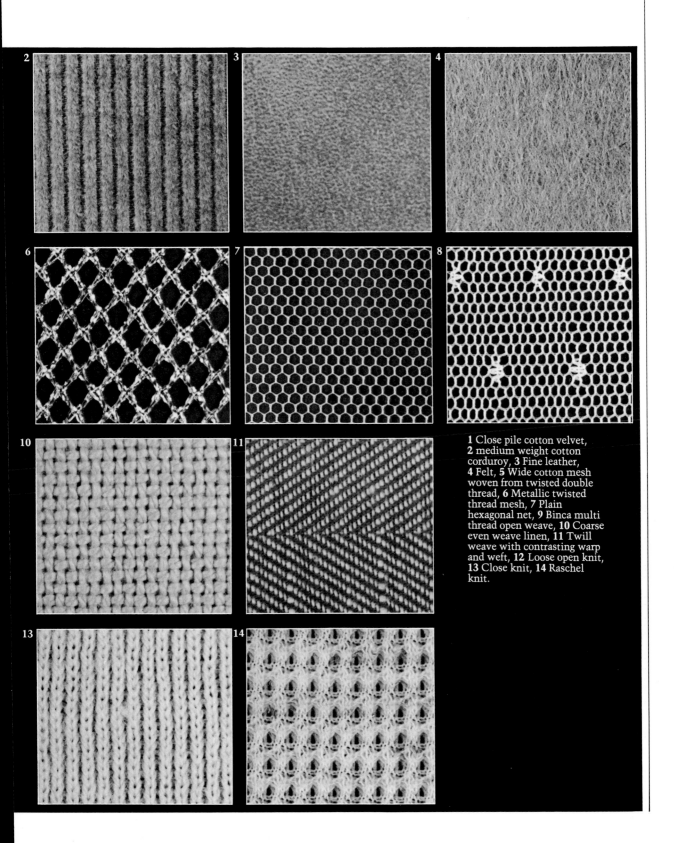

1 Close pile cotton velvet, 2 medium weight cotton corduroy, 3 Fine leather, 4 Felt, 5 Wide cotton mesh woven from twisted double thread, 6 Metallic twisted thread mesh, 7 Plain hexagonal net, 9 Binca multi thread open weave, 10 Coarse even weave linen, 11 Twill weave with contrasting warp and weft, 12 Loose open knit, 13 Close knit, 14 Raschel knit.

Qualities of fabrics

By collecting and comparing as many fabrics as possible you will learn their different qualities, and, almost certainly, personal preferences will start to develop. Try combining fabrics that are similar in colour to make use of the varying effects of light on the surface.

Consider the direction of the pile of velvet and corduroy and observe the apparent tonal change that takes place at different angles.

Think about fabrics that have a different colour warp and weft, such as Thai silk. Again there is a rich variety of tone and colour to be seen and exploited in the single piece of fabric.

Consider the use of transparent fabrics, exploring the change of tone and colour which can be achieved by layering one fabric on another.

To gain further appreciation of the exciting potential of the many types of fabric, try disturbing the surface and structure: firstly by displacing the threads, then removing them altogether, making holes, cutting, tearing and fraying edges so that the fabric is entirely altered. Obviously different constructions will react differently to these treatments, and you will learn how a certain fabric will suit a certain embroidery technique. Some fabrics are particularly amenable to a variety of techniques, and so become dependable favourites.

In a single-colour design the use of these contrasts of surfaces produces different tones and added interest. A small experimental piece exploring these tactile qualities can be the starting point for a larger scale work. BELOW: An abstract collage of fabrics illustrating the variety of surfaces and textures available to the embroiderer. Smooth surfaces contrast with rough ones, and shiny with matt finishes.

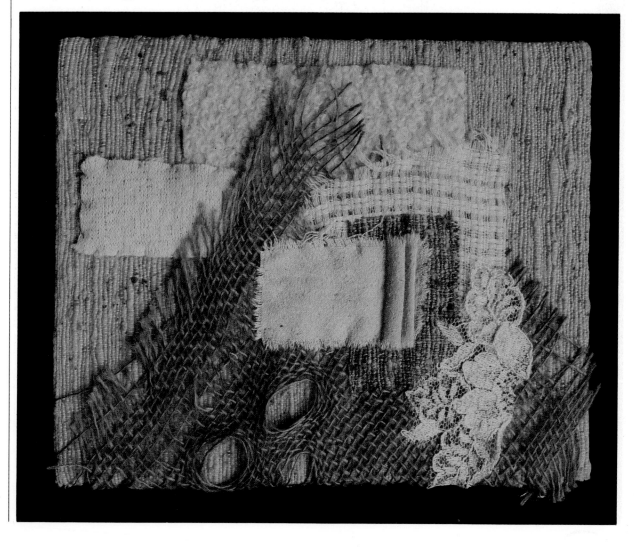

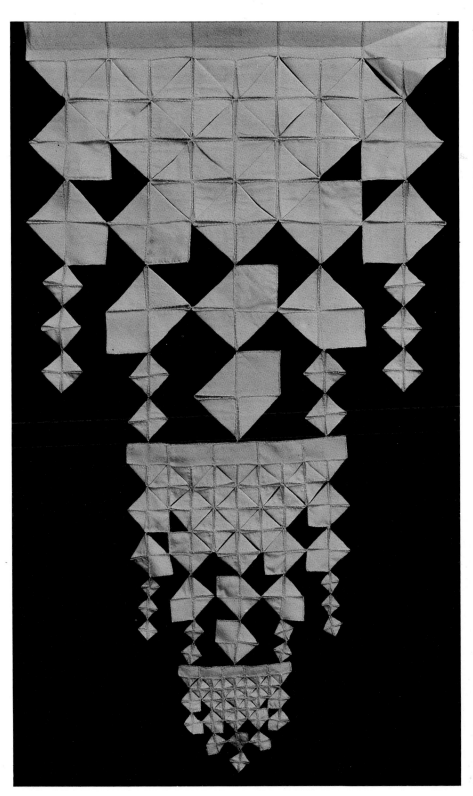

A single fabric can be folded and manipulated in a variety of ways to produce many different effects.
LEFT: This hanging is made entirely of calico, based on a design of geometric forms. Square units are folded with envelope shapes of varying sizes. These are joined together at angles and hung from bars of fabric starting with the larger ones at the top, graduating in size to rows of small ones eventually finishing in a single unit forming a point.

DYEING FABRICS

Sometimes it can be difficult to find the right fabric in the right colour, while you are continually discarding pieces of fabric that have accumulated in the cupboard as being unsuitable. The solution is to use some of the excellent dyes that are available today. The easiest ones to experiment with are the cold water (or fibre-reactive) dyes, which are suitable for cotton, linen, silk, rayon and wool, but not nylon, acrylic or polyester. The small tins of dye, which can be bought from most departmental stores, will dye 8oz (226gm) of dry fabric. It is advisable to wear rubber gloves when using dye.

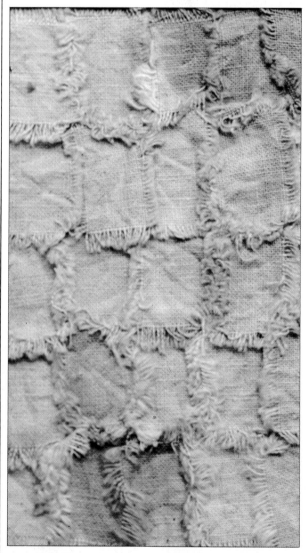

ABOVE: *Small squares of coarse cotton are space-dyed in pink and blue and then pieced together. The rough frayed edges of each piece make a feature in this experimental sample and complement the free effect achieved by this method of dyeing.*

Techniques
Before you begin to dye, it is advisable to cover the work surface with newspaper and remember to keep the utensils you use for dyeing purposes only.

To help the dye penetrate the fibres and make it permanent, the dyed fabric is soaked in separate solutions of salt and soda. The fabric to be dyed should first be thoroughly washed. This will remove any dressing from new fabrics and detergent from those which have been previously washed.

Prepare the salt solution by dissolving 4ozs (113gm) of cooking salt in 16fl ozs (1.78 litres) of water. Make the soda solution by dissolving 2ozs (56gm) of household soda in 8fl ozs (0.89 litres) of warm water, and put both solutions to one side.

Following the manufacturer's instructions, dissolve the dye powder in cold water, put into a bucket, and stir well. Immerse the wet fabric and agitate for five minutes. Leave for ten minutes for the dye to penetrate the fibres. Remove the fabric and add the salt solution, stir and replace the fabric. Stir frequently for 15 minutes while the salt drives the dye into the fibres. Remove the fabric again, add the soda solution, stir and replace the fabric. Stir well and leave for at least one hour, stirring every 15 minutes while the soda fixes the dye. Remove the fabric and pour away the dye. Rinse until the water is clear and then wash in hot soapy water, rinse well and dry. The depth of colour depends on the ratio of dye powder to fabric, so experiment with varying quantities to achieve dark or pale colours. Also try mixing two or more colours together in varying proportions to obtain new colours.

Space Dyeing
Whereas conventional dyeing gives dependable and repeatable colours, this method will give a different result every single time. Changes in the combination and proportion of dye colours used will give an endless series of effects. Threads can be dyed at the same time as the fabrics. Tie them in loose hanks to stop tangling.

Dye applied in this way will give the fabric a random, multicoloured effect. The most effective method is as follows: prepare the fabric, soda and salt solutions as before. Lay pieces or strips of fabric in a large plastic container such as a cat litter tray. Choose two or three contrasting colours and mix one third of each tin separately as before, and put them into jam jars. Fill jam jars with salt solution. Using each jar separately, spoon the dye at random over the fabric in the tray. Press the fabric down so that it is covered by the solution, but do not agitate as the colours will mix too much. Leave for ten minutes then pour soda solution evenly over the fabric. Leave for 30 minutes, then rinse as before.

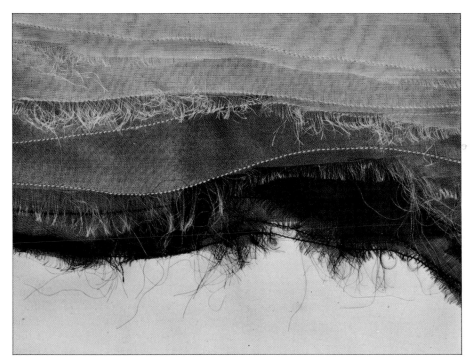

LEFT: *A delicate shadowy effect is created by over-lapping transparent fabric of varying tones. The attractive frayed edges contrast with the machined lines used for piecing the work together. Tones of one colour can be obtained by varying the strength of the dye used and also varying the length of time for immersing the fabric.*

BELOW: *A wide range of fabrics including muslin, silk, chiffon and organza are space-dyed with a range of colours to achieve a multi-coloured effect. These fabrics are pieced together in a free interpretation of the log cabin technique with gathered and ruched fabric to form the centre squares.*

DESIGNING

What exactly is meant by design? It means to make an arrangement, to plan and select ingredients that will work together as a whole. What precisely makes a good design as opposed to a poor design is difficult to define. Purpose and personal taste play an integral part. This is apparent in an individual's personal style, choice of clothes and home environment. The elements of colour, line, space and form all play an important part in the composition of a design.

Designing begins with a purpose, whether it is to decorate clothing, to enhance a particular piece of fabric or to develop an idea inspired by something seen or experienced. From this starting-point, the process of design goes through several phases, beginning with collecting information, continuing with discarding and selecting ideas, and going on to explore different ways of working in a search for the most effective means of projecting the idea.

Inspiration

Inspiration is received through the senses, from literally touching surfaces, hearing a piece of music; but most of all through observation. You must make yourself visually aware of the shapes and patterns around you; both those in nature, and those in something as artificial as a supermarket. (Notice stacked tins, lines of trolleys, queues of people.) Look for texture and colour; in the kitchen, notice the peelings of vegetables, broken eggshells, arrangments of china. Many painters have made the everyday beautiful, at different periods; look at seventeenth-century Dutch paintings, or the domestic interiors of the Frenchman Édouard Vuillard (1868-1940). In this same vein might be such works as a group of bricks, displayed at the Tate Gallery in London.

BELOW LEFT: *A rubbing of wood grain, made with wax crayon on paper.*

BELOW: *Selected lines from the rubbing, worked in thick and fine threads.*

Collecting and Selecting

Factual information can be recorded by making notes, simple drawings, diagrams and by collecting or taking photographs. From this information a selection can be made and the actual design can begin to take shape on paper. The method of designing is a personal preference; but small 'thumbnail' sketches will help to get the plan started. As you sketch, select samples of fabrics and threads; you are effectively making a palette from which to work. By taking different areas of the design and working small samples in fabric and thread, many problems can be resolved before the larger-scale work is tackled. It will quickly become apparent which are the most effective, and these can be used as a reference for the final piece of work.

When you are faced with a complicated shape, such as for instance a plant with many overlapping leaves, it will be helpful to make an outline drawing, treating the subject as a shadow cast upon a wall. You can add details within this simplified shape. Do not forget that the spaces between the leaves, as revealed in the drawing, may also be made into a feature of the design.

Of all the ways of collecting information, drawing is the most immediate and useful. A simple diagram is often all that is needed to record an idea. Those who 'can't draw' need not despair; everyone can draw to some extent, and can certainly make marks. Children match marks to images in a lively and instinctive way.

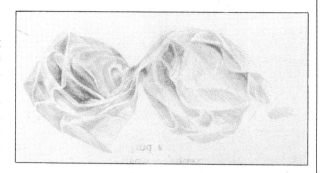

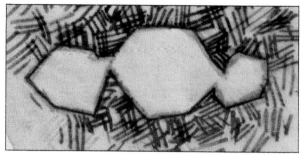

This drawing of a wrapped sweet (top) was traced to simplify the shape and give a strong outline. The tracing was transferred to calico for experiments for colouring and developing the background in felt pen and thread (centre). The final design (below) repeats the outline of the sweet motif; blocks of satin stitch in coton à broder fill the spaces between the shapes.

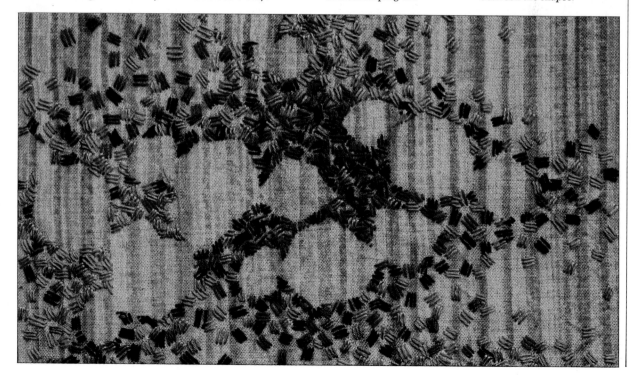

In addition to the use of a sketch book, a camera is a useful way of recording interesting shapes and textures. Experiment by photographing objects from unusual angles, reflected images, silhouettes and structural details. A photograph makes a good starting point for a simple design — whether you use an image from a magazine or one you have taken yourself. Choose one which features strong lines, simple shapes and contrasting tones. Make a view-finder by cutting two L-shapes from paper or thin card; move these around to frame a suitable area to develop a design. Using tracing paper, trace the main lines within the selected area to give the basic structure and guidelines for the embroidery. Transfer the design onto a plain-coloured background fabric with a firm smooth weave.

In this example, a photograph of ivy leaves provides the basic idea for a simple design worked in cutwork. Several tracings are taken before choosing one to develop. The shapes are simplified and then enlarged to make a suitable motif for the chosen technique, bearing in mind that areas of the background will be cut away. The larger solid area is balanced by the smaller negative shapes of the cutwork. Several designs may be developed from the same basic idea and it is useful to keep all the tracings for future reference.

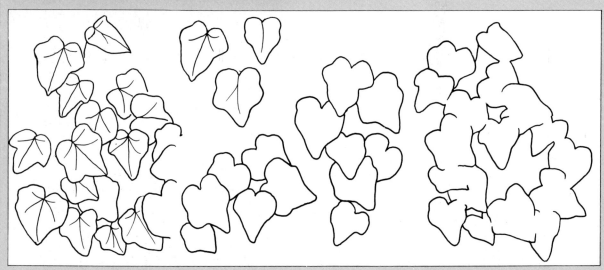

AS A STARTING POINT

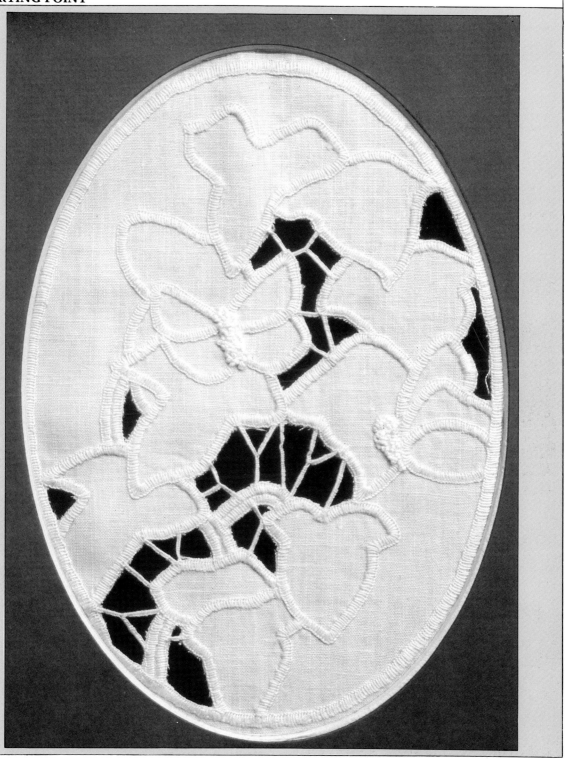

Mark-making

Mark-making is the basis of drawing; most people 'doodle' without inhibition. Doodles flow out from thoughts unconsciously or absent-mindedly. Drawing is a way of thinking, searching and visualizing, but, like playing the piano, it needs practice to increase experience and confidence. The range of mark-making is not confined to one kind of pencil and paper; try applying inks, crayons, chalks and paints to a variety of surfaces like textured papers, tissue paper, blotting paper, acetate sheet, and even fabric. Drawing tools can include pens, brushes, sticks, sponges, fingers, strips of card, in fact anything that will make a mark.

Monoprinting is an extension of mark-making. Use such objects as corks, cotton reels, and small pieces of wood as printing blocks. Brush them with paint and press them down firmly onto paper or cloth. Use this method to explore pattern-making. Compare a pattern built up by repetition of one unit with a random printing of various units. How could they be interpreted in stitches?

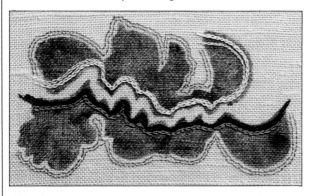

ABOVE: *This flower design has been simplified by taking a tracing from which a stencil has been cut. Fabric paint and a stencil brush are used to transfer the design onto the background fabric. Lines of stitching emphasize these shapes.*

BELOW: *The solid shape cut away from the stencil is used as a template to make a further design. In this exercise, the outlines are vignetted and the uneven edges enriched with stitching in blackwork patterns. The shapes are decorated with lines of stem stitch.*

USING A STENCIL

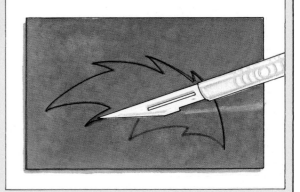

1 Begin by drawing your motif on thin card. Then, working on a cutting board, cut out the shape (with a scalpel), cutting carefully away from the corners.

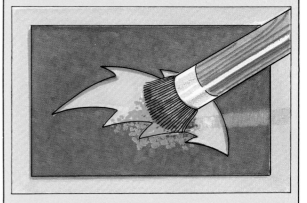

2 Holding the stencil firmly in place, fill cut out shape with colour, holding the stencil brush upright and dapping with the flat end of the bristles.

3 Leave the first colour to dry before replacing the stencil, overlapping part of the motif. Fill with colour, noting darker area where motifs overlap.

DESIGNING WITH PAPER

Cut simple repeating patterns from folded paper; coloured gummed squares are particularly effective. Note that the negative shapes of the remaining paper make a design in their own right. Arrange your cut shapes on to a background sheet; place them in lines, squares, circles, semi-circles, triangles, or at random.

Repeat the exercise using coloured tissue paper. This time use the additional possibility of designing with overlapping colours.

Tearing paper instead of cutting it gives a different quality, as does tearing instead of cutting fabric. Make a collage of various types of paper, both cut and torn. This is an excellent way of designing in shapes, and is particularly suitable for a design to be carried out in appliqué. Treat the exercise as a transition between a complex drawing and a final design for embroidery; it simplifies the shapes, and gives an indication of the order in which to work the processes and stitches.

Now introduce the third dimension. Cut strips of paper and weave them together to form a new design. Newsprint treated in this way will give tonal patterns; photographs from magazines, or drawings, will give distorted images.

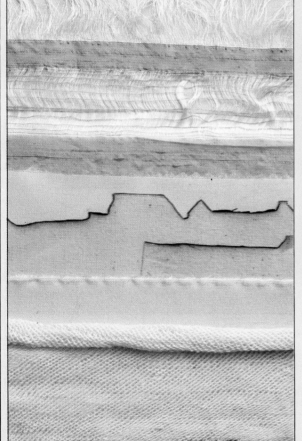

Try twisting your paper strips as you weave them, or loop them to give a highly diverse surface. Further three-dimensional effects can be obtained by folding, creasing, and crumpling paper. Bear in mind the arts of origami and paper sculpture. These can be used to make a maquette for a textile structure or a three-dimensional form.

TOP: *Different papers are woven to form an uneven grid.*

ABOVE: *A stitched sample on corduroy in bands of couched wool and herringbone stitch.*

LEFT: *A similar exercise is developed using layers of silk, cotton and knitted fabric whose edges are frayed, pinked, torn and singed and folded.*

LOOKING AT LINES

Line, shape, form and tone are the classic elements of design, but it can be argued that line is the basis from which the others develop. The many different qualities of line dictate the message it conveys. Lines make edges, enclose shapes, accentuate forms and, when repeated close together, create tone. Straight vertical lines have a static architectural quality, while horizontal lines suggest a flat, calm landscape. Curving lines convey movement and direction, and diagonal lines create tension. The sinuous, pliant lines of the Art Nouveau period (1890s-1900s) give a feeling of movement and growth, contrasting with the angular geometric lines of the Art Deco style which followed (1920s-30s). The latter echoed the modern age of mechanization and functional design.

The painter William Hogarth (1697-1764) talks about the 'line of beauty', a serpentine curve like the letter S, in his book *The Analysis of Beauty*:

'The eye hath this sort of enjoyment in winding walks, and serpentine rivers, and all sorts of objects, whose forms, as we shall see hereafter, are composed of what, I call, the waving and serpentine lines. Intricacy in form therefore I shall define to be that peculiarity in the lines, which compose it, that leads the eye a wanton kind of chance, and from the pleasure that gives the mind, intitles it to the name of beautiful…'

The Swiss artist Paul Klee (1879-1940) talks about 'taking a line for a walk', which immediately conjures up the image of a meandering path crossing and turning, leading the eye in and around the picture.

ABOVE: *The exterior reflected in the window is divided into a grid by the frame giving an abstract quality which can be used as a basis for a design. The worked example is based* *on rectangular shapes using rice stitch in various weights of thread.*

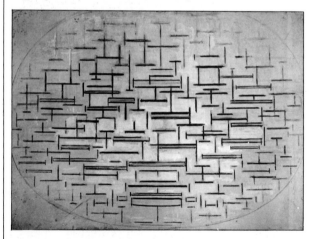

ABOVE: *The painting by Piet Mondrian 'The Sea' basically a simple use of vertical and horizontal lines. An illusion of movement and space is created by varying weights and lengths of line which seem to undulate. The* *eye is led in and around through a labyrinth of spaces.*

Quality of Line

A line can be continuous or broken, thick or thin, jagged or flowing, shiny or matt, blurred or precise, even or uneven, open or closed. It varies in character as it moves in a direction or around a shape. Consider how the grain lines of wood change as they flow through the form. The threads and stitches selected in embroidery influence the linear character of the work. The meeting of horizontal and vertical lines leads into structures; making a division of space and proportion suggesting architecture. Where lines cross, the eye is arrested and tension is created. This intersection of lines gives mathematical grids on one side and organic systems on the other. Consider scaffolding, veining in leaves, and bare branches of trees against the skyline.

MOVEMENT IN LINE

Curving lines convey movement of many kinds. They can swirl and twist forming exciting and disturbing rhythms, or rise and fall in gentle sinuous flowing forms. Of all line formations the spiral gives the most feeling of movement and space; it can be used in design to suggest air, water, fire, light and infinity. Look at rising smoke, ripples in water, tendrils, a spiral staircase, and nautilus shells. When lines join as a circle they contain a space, give continuity and create form. Diagonal lines give direction, and when brought together with horizontals and verticals they form intricate patterns, and straight lines can appear to become curves; for instance a parabola, honeycombs in nature and Islamic patterns. Horizontal lines have a tranquility and repose. When emphasized they give stability to a design. Skylines, landscape and strata are all instances where the relationship between horizontals gives a sense of mood and space. Vertical lines can suggest growth or a sense of distance; for example, posts and figures in a street.

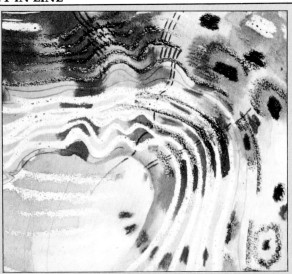

RIGHT: *A drawing using wax resist and colour washes giving a rippling effect.*

BELOW: *Textured fabric and curved edges combine to achieve a similar effect.*

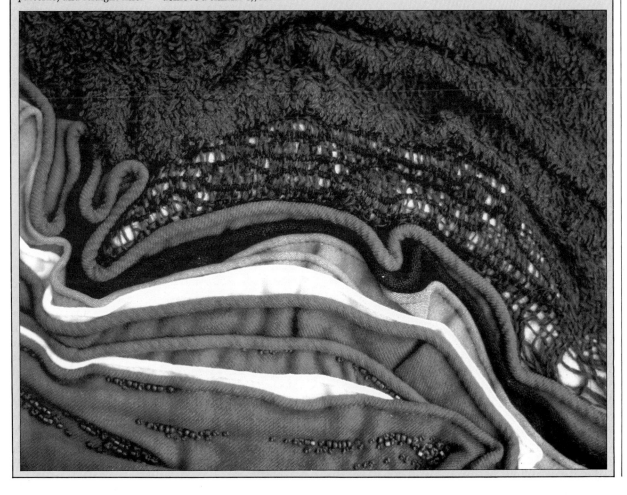

ABOVE: *The design for this panel is based on the strata of the Grand Canyon in Arizona. The sun and shadows on the layers create subtle differences in color. Rows of straight stitches are worked in tones of rust and purple, to interpret this effect. The embroidery is worked in fine silk thread on a background of handwoven silk.*

RIGHT: *The pattern of rock strata is explored in this sampler of pekinese stitch, which is worked in a wide variety of threads. The change of spacing between the lines, and the scale and texture of the stitches, gives the feeling of strength and movement.*

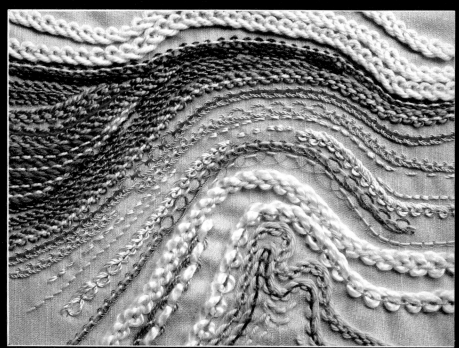

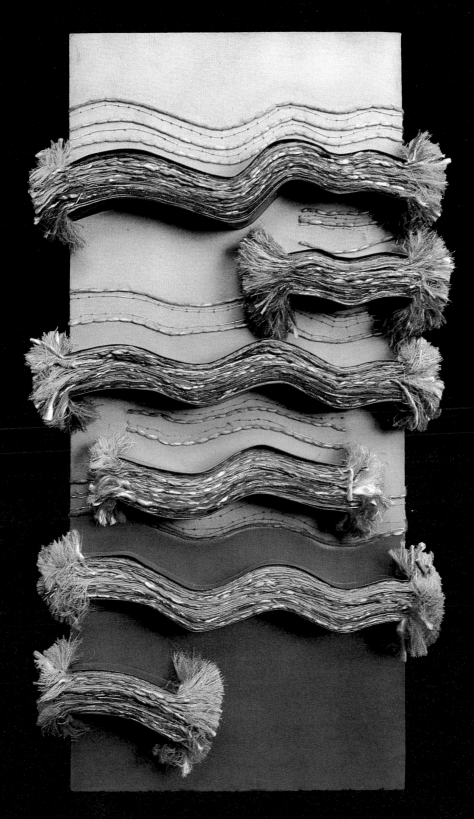

LEFT: *Dyed fabrics and threads, ranging from deep blue, through shades of green to pale yellow are used for this panel. The three-dimensional effect is achieved by one-inch deep bands of metal which enclose folded fabrics at right angles to the background. The strata effect is made by the curving shapes of the metal bands and by the graded color of the folded fabrics. The background fabric has been spray-dyed in shaded color, and lines of couched threads have been stitched to accentuate the linear qualities of the design. The finished panel has been stretched over a board, slightly smaller than the bands across, to create a sharp contrast between the hard edge of the board and the soft tufts of thread.*

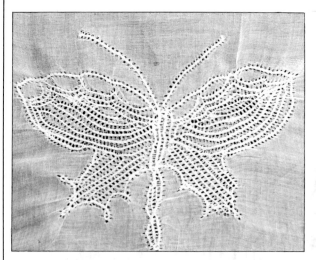

ABOVE: *The linear patterns on a butterfly's wings in machine-stitched pulled work contrast with the fine* organdie background. ABOVE RIGHT: *Vertical, horizontal, and diagonal stitches worked singly* and sometimes overlapped, to create depth and texture. BELOW: *The swirls and rhythms of marbling,* emphasized by lines of chain stitch. Variations in spacing add extra interest.

LOOKING AT INTERIORS

Simple house interiors can suggest many ideas for embroidery design. The staircase has an uncluttered geometric structure.

Make some simple sketches at different times of day, noting how the shadows fall *(top)*. The pattern on the staircarpet could be an important part of the composition.

Try sitting in a darkened hallway or corridor with a glimpse into a brightly lit room or down a flight of stairs from a landing. You will see a composition, with a colourful focal point surrounded by a darker frame. A corner of a familiar room may be seen in an unfamiliar way by viewing it in a mirror. Try the mirror at various angles to the vertical and the horizontal; this will yield an interesting collection of shapes and patterns. Be careful to select only those details useful for the composition. Studies of doors, windows, arches and gates and photographs from furnishing magazines will provide further ideas.

In this piece of embroidery striped materials are used for the horizontal and vertical lines, and ribbon applied for the strong diagonal of the handrail, which quickly takes the eye up to the landing. Details have been added with machine stitchery, and surrounded with further strips of striped cotton. The piece could be one of a series of quilt blocks on the same theme, joined together using a log cabin patchwork technique.

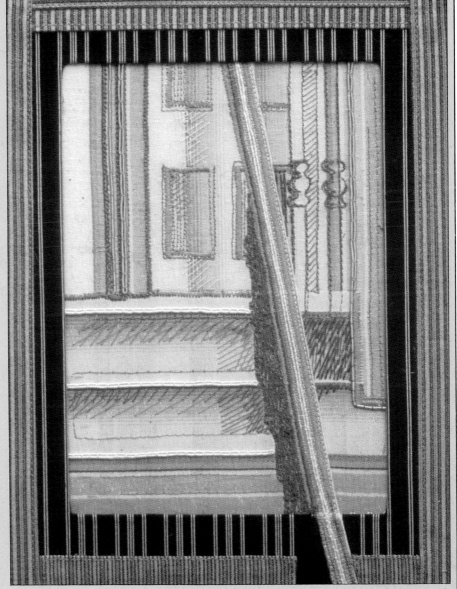

WORKING WITH COLOUR

Choosing the background fabric and then spilling out a selection of threads in various colourways can be an exciting way to start work. In embroidery the initial stimulation comes not only from colour, but also from the subtle nuances brought about by the variety of fabrics and threads, their textures and fibres. Consider the rich lustre of pure silk, the softness of mohair, the mixed colours of tweed, and the fall of light on the pile of velvet. Much has been written about colour theory, and certain principles can be learned, but in practice the choice of colour is a matter of personal decision.

Colour is relative

As the Victorian art critic John Ruskin said: 'Every line throughout your work is altered by every touch that you add in other places; so that what was warm a minute ago, becomes colder when you have put a hotter colour in another place, and what was harmony when you left it, becomes discordant as you set other colours beside it.'

Colours can be grouped in the following categories: warm to cool, dark to light, dull to bright. A pink can either be warm with a yellow cast, or cool with a blue cast. It will appear dark with lighter colours or light with dark intense colours. In addition the proportion in which the colour is used will affect its impact. Fragmentation of one colour with another will appear to make the two merge; larger areas of colour will remain separate.

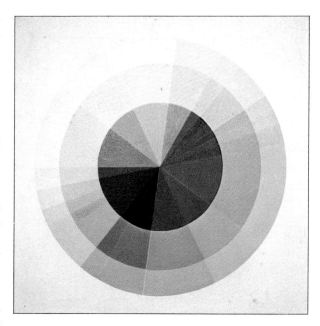

ABOVE: *This interpretation of Seurat's colour wheel from a painting by Bridget Riley is based on the three primary colours, red, blue and yellow. When two of these are combined, secondary colours are produced. From this simple starting point, the endless kaleidoscope of colour is formed. The basic colours, can be diffused by adding black, grey or white.*

LEFT: *A panel based on drawings and colour observations of the leaves of a coleas plant. The complementary colours of red and green are explored for their intensity and tonal qualities. The embroidery is worked on an evenweave background fabric, in blocks of straight stitches, using twisted silk threads.*

RIGHT: *This piece of canvaswork is inspired by the multi-colour effect of flowers in a border. The central area is worked in rice stitch, the main cross of which is worked in various colours of floss rayon. The crossed corners are all worked in green coton à broder. The cushion stitch border and the double green frame echo the pinks and greens of the centre.*

Observing colour

In the view from a window throughout the day from dawn to dusk, the colours will intensify and even appear to change as they are affected by the quality of light. Cloudy skies diffuse colour; and this is particularly noticeable in the English landscape, affected as it is by the vagaries of the weather. In contrast to this, the cloudless skies of California make the colours appear pure and intense. The quality of light influences the people's choice of clothes; bright blues, yellows, pinks, reds and greens which may look right under sunny skies look out of place in a grey and cloudy environment.

Observe the proportions of colours and their relationships in colour schemes to be found in nature and man-made objects. These range from such familiar examples as flowers, butterflies, fruit and foliage, to the less obvious ones found in rusting tins, peeling paint, rubbish heaps, and other improbable situations.

The impromptu colour schemes formed by groups of people in the street, posters on a hoarding, goods on a market stall or in a shop window can suggest exciting and unusual relationships. The mixed, bright colours and overlapping shapes of strings of flags, bunches of balloons, deckchairs on a promenade all add to the endless source of inspiration from the world around us.

TOP AND ABOVE: *A photograph of a compost heap provides the unusual inspiration for a small panel embroidered completely in freely-worked cross stitch. The layers of colour, tone and texture are explored using a wide variety of threads and strips of fabric.*

RIGHT AND FAR RIGHT: *Drawings provide an equally useful method of recording shapes, colours, tones and patterns. This drawing of plants in a herb garden is developed into a panel using applied layers of fine fabric and a variety of threads to interpret the subtle range of colours.*

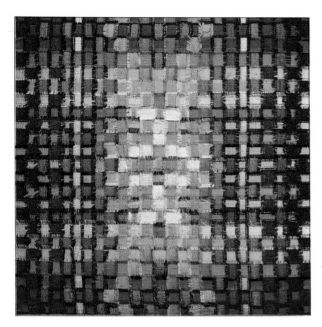

Mood and movement of colour

With the whole spectrum from which to choose many moods can be encompassed. Pure hues are lively, pale harmonious tones, tranquil. Discordant colours create tension and disturb the eye. The juxtaposition of strong colours can produce a dazzling effect, almost seeming to move, as in the paintings of Bridget Riley. A three-dimensional look can be contrived by gradations of colour on a flat surface; light colours on a dark ground will tend to come forward and *vice versa*. Warm colours usually come forward and cool ones retreat, pure colours will tend to advance relative to duller ones. Study the geometric paintings of Victor Vasèrely, the French-Hungarian artist. He uses colour and tonal relationships to create an illusion of depth and movement.

LEFT: *Closely worked French knots give rich colour to a background.*

ABOVE: *Frayed strips of silks are woven to make a grid of shimmering colour.*

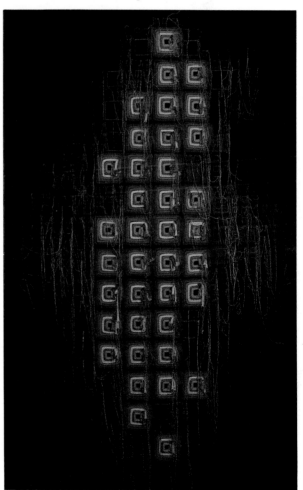

LEFT: *Subtle tones of grey-green create the illusion of distance. Broken edges merge one tone with another.*

ABOVE: *A black backgound used as a foil for complimentary colours. The embroidery is machine-stitched.*

Tonal values

The balance of tone is just as important as the balance of colour in a design. It can be most easily checked by looking through half-closed eyes.

The natural tonal order of colours, from the lightest yellow to the deepest purple, can be extended by the addition of white, grey or black to pure colours. This creates new tones and shades and these will vary depending on how much paint is added, and can even reverse the natural order. Purple can become a pale lilac with the addition of white; a rich mustard yellow can be derived by adding grey to the original bright yellow.

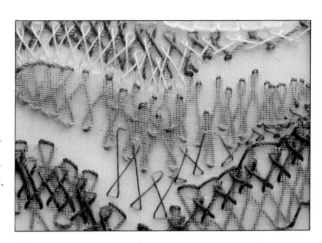

RIGHT: *The shadows of herringbone stitch worked in different thicknesses on a transparent fabric extend the subtlety of the tonal values.*

The expressive marks of graphite on paper, as in a pencil drawing, can be used to record a very wide range of tonal values. The more subtle middle tones are used in this drawing of a spray of mimosa flowers. The pale flowers are silhouetted against the darker marks of the leaves.

The pencil drawing is freely translated into a delicate piece of embroidery, using back, straight and satin stitches, which relate to the soft, feathery quality of the original flowers and leaves. Variety of tone is achieved by working some stitches closely and others further apart.

This design of buildings is worked out on isometric graph paper in pen and ink. Cross-hatching is used in addition to outlining, to achieve gradations of tone which give the illusion of three-dimensional form.

By varying the spacing between the lines of cross-hatching — and also the thickness of the line — a wide range of tone can be suggested.

The blackwork technique is ideally suited to carry out this design in stitchery. Tone can be built up by the use of different thicknesses of thread, ranging from fine sewing cotton, silk twist, coton à broder to coton perlé, and by varying the stitch patterns. The many gradations of tone built up in this way give interest and variety to the embroidery.

LEFT: *Dye and transparent fabrics are applied to the background fabric. Hand embroidery in straight stitches and French knots build up the design, emphasizing the subtle greens and mauves. A hint of blue and red adds a final highlight of colour.*

ABOVE: *This example uses a foundation of applied pieces of transparent fabrics. Flower motifs in machine-stitched embroidery are worked over the surface. The colours used are similar to the hand-stitched example, but touches of yellow and viridian add richness to the subtle greens.*

BELOW: *The bright primary and secondary colours of the hot-air balloons and their geometric patterns are translated with stitchery. The embroidery is worked in silks on a silk background.*

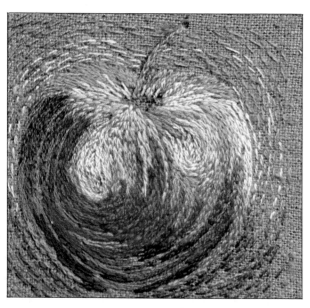

ABOVE: *An apple worked in running and split stitches The use of colour and direction of line emphasize the roundness of the form.*

MIXING OF TONES

Build up motifs by intermingling subtle tones of different colours.

A magazine cutting inspired the drawing and embroidery of an eye. It is worked entirely in French knots, in threads of varying thicknesses.

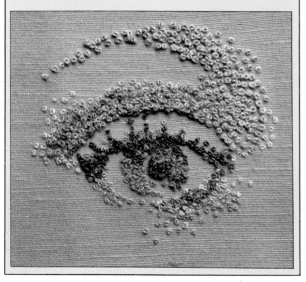

ABOVE: *In this picture, the bright colours of flowers in a herbaceous border intermingle with softer, darker colours of the shadows of the foliage. The background fabric is coloured with transfer paints and then overlaid in areas with coloured gauzes. The colour is emphasized with bright silk threads in simple straight and knotted stitches.*

STITCHING ON EVENWEAVE
BLACKWORK

It is said that Catherine of Aragon brought blackwork from Spain when she married Henry VIII in 1509, but black counted-thread embroidery on a white ground was practised in England before that date. Originally it was used for dress decoration, particularly on the very full sleeves of women's dresses. It can be seen in Tudor portraits by Hans Holbein (1497-1543) and George Gower (c1516-85); but it soon came to be used for a wider range of domestic items, including bed-hangings, cushions and curtains. By the beginning of the seventeenth century, blackwork was used with more freedom, and a greater variety of stitches. Designs varied from the pictorial to geometric patterns, from isolated natural motifs to continuous scrolling leaves and flowers. Many of the geometric designs show Arabic influence; fillings for leaf and flower motifs are similar to those of needlepoint lace. Isolated plant designs were influenced by the botanical woodcuts which illustrated contemporary herbals.

Blackwork was largely a monochrome technique, usually in black thread on a white ground, but sometimes red thread was used, and gold and silver thread might have been added for richness.

During the first half of this century, blackwork embroiderers kept closely to traditional stitch patterns, outlining each section carefully with chain, whipped chain, stem or back stitch; as a result, they made tight designs with little freedom to experiment. Today, although traditional stitch patterns are usually followed, to maintain the character of the technique, it is acceptable to invent or adapt them to achieve broader effects of texture, mood and contrast. Outlining is no longer obligatory; line can be used in conjunction with mass, and other techniques, such as appliqué, free stitchery and canvaswork stitches, can be added. When used pictorially, blackwork images are built up of varying blocks of contrast and tonal values to create three-dimensional effects.

ABOVE: Example of blackwork dating from the sixteenth century. The design is outlined in couched metal threads, and the shapes are filled with blackwork patterns embroidered in fine silk on an evenweave linen.

RIGHT: A modern panel based on a design of figures in action. Threads in different thicknesses are used to build up a variation in tone, and are emphasized by the interplay of stitch patterns.

Notice that the figures in the central section are unworked areas. Their shapes are created by the patterned background. The contrast between these and the figures either side provides an interesting example of counterchange.

Holbein stitch is a variation of double running stitch. Begin as for double running stitch making a series of short even stitches on traced line. Turn work around and work running stitces in spaces. To work offshoot stitches, bring needle out on line, make a short right angle stitch bringing needle out at starting point ready to continue stitching (**2**). Complete row, turn work and fill spaces as before (**3**).

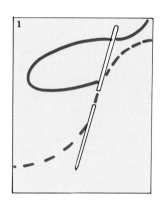
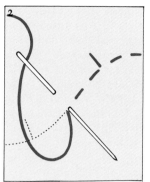
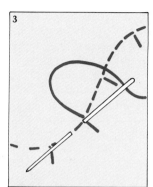

Technique

The two basic stitches for blackwork are double-running or Holbein stitch (called after the sixteenth-century painter) and back stitch. Holbein stitch produces a smoother line, and reduces the tendency to distort the fabric by pulling the thread too tight. Back stitch is sometimes appropriate; both stitches can be used in one piece of work.

These stitches are used to build up traditional patterns, which are repeated for borders, fillings, or blocks of tone. It is possible to modify a stitch pattern to fill the shapes in a design, so that outlining is unnecessary (except for emphasis or clarity); but a combination of line and blocks of stitches is effective.

Start each pattern with two or three back stitches, which will then be worked over. Avoid long stitches on the back, which may show through as a shadow.

MATERIALS

Fabrics should be evenweave linen or cotton, loosely or closely woven, with easily countable threads. Choose fabrics in accordance with the effect you want: lawn for very fine work, 'square' net for interesting transparent effects. Hessian, canvas or regularly woven tweeds can be used for bold designs, if suitable thread is selected. Other fabrics can be applied as required.
Needles For fine work, use size 26 tapestry needles; size 18 for coarse work. Avoid sharp-pointed needles, as these are liable to split the thread of the fabric.
Threads Use tacking thread of a contrasting colour for transferring the design. For the work itself, a range of thicknesses from 60 machine silk to number 8 or 5 coton perlé may be used. A smooth thread, which maintains the precision of the stitch pattern, is most effective. If free stitchery is introduced, thicker threads may be used; but textured threads, if used, must be couched down. With coarse work, knitting wools, coton à broder, strings, and heavy coton perlé are appropriate. Traditionally, the thread should be black or red, but experiment with tones of one colour, a combination of two or three colours, or a light colour on a dark ground.

When using a range of black threads, add a fine grey thread, to extend the lightest tone.

DESIGN IN MONOCHROME

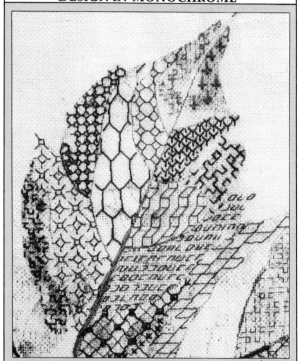

It is important to see a design in terms of areas of tone, without unnecessary detail. Look at a photograph with half closed eyes, for example. Tracing and tacking is a simple way of transferring this type of design. Alternatively ink an object, for example a leaf, and press it on to the fabric. This gives an irregular outline on which to build. Establish an overall idea of tone values before concentrating on detail. Areas of lighter and darker tone are built up with fine or thick threads, or light or dense stitch patterns. Dark areas can be worked into later. Perspective, depth and overlapping are achieved by control of the stiches. Stiches worked on a large scale, with thick thread, come forward, while less detailed, smaller stitches in fine thread will recede.

This piece of embroidery was worked from a design taken from an ink impression of a leaf.

CANVASWORK

Canvaswork has a long history. Some stitches which are today almost exclusively associated with canvaswork have been known for hundreds of years; originally they would have been worked on evenweave linen. Historically, the most popular stitch is tent stitch. The name comes form the French *tenter* - 'to stretch'; it refers to stretching the background fabric on a frame for working. Fine tent stitch appears on pieces from the middle ages; during the reign of Elizabeth I it was used for furnishings, bags, pin-cushions and book covers. Tent stitch hangings closely resemble tapestry (woven on a loom), for which they made an excellent substitute. Much of the work came from professional workshops but a great deal was done at home.

Canvaswork furnishings again became popular towards the end of the seventeenth century. Examples of furniture upholstered with canvaswork survive from the seventeenth century; many can be seen in stately homes in their original setting. Canvaswork was also used for smaller pieces, such as polescreens and pocket books.

Berlin woolwork

Very early in the nineteenth century coloured charts, published in Berlin, began to be imported into Britain, together with wools and canvas for working them. Eventually 'Berlin woolwork' and 'canvaswork' became synonymous. By the 1830s it became a craze which swept Britain (and later the USA). Slippers, bags, cushions, upholstery and innumerable small items were produced.

Tent and cross stitch were still popular; there was also a form of raised pile (sometimes called plushwork) which gave a three-dimensional effect. Beads were often incorporated. Another trend was the copying of popular Victorian paintings in canvaswork. Although much of the early work was charming, and Berlin woolwork samplers contain many delightful patterns, the introduction of chemical dyes in the mid-century led to the use of harsh, strident colours and design deteriorated. With the changes in taste which followed the work of William Morris and his followers, Berlin woolwork lost ground, though its echoes are still with us today.

ABOVE: *A typical example of Berlin woolwork — the central motif from a late nineteenth-century cushion cover. Rose and floral designs were extremely popular during this period; many charts showing similar designs, which were given away with women's magazines, survive. This piece is worked in wool, on a double thread linen canvas, in tent stitch. A small section of the canvas can be seen on the white rose.*

LEFT: *The Finding of Moses, an early seventeenth-century panel. Biblical and allegorical subjects were often used at this time. The panel is worked in tent stitch with a fine silk thread on canvas; the colours are shaded to give form to the subjects.*

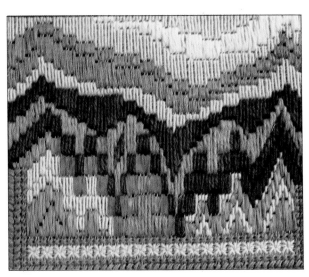

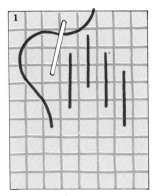

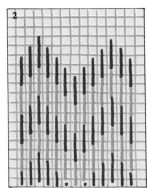

ABOVE: *A free interpretation of Florentine stitch worked in string, cord, raffia and strips of leather on rug canvas.*

Florentine stitch is worked on single canvas and gives a pronounced zigzag effect. Bring needle out and make three straight stitches upwards over three threads and back two. Then work two stitches downwards in reverse sequence and repeat to row end (**1**). There are many variations where the stitch sequences are changed to make longer or shorter zigzag patterns, and usually worked in shaded colours to give a 'flame' effect (**2**).

Canvaswork today

It seems that canvaswork never completely loses its appeal. Perhaps the regularity of the traditional stitches has a therapeutic quality. (Canvaswork was in fact used in the First World War as therapy for shell-shocked soldiers.) Many people make their first attempt at embroidery through a canvaswork 'kit', and from there progress to making their own designs. Canvaswork may now be combined with other techniques in experimental work. A variety of threads and materials are used together; stitches other than canvaswork stitches are included; parts of the canvas may be left unworked or may be painted.

MATERIALS

There are two kinds of canvas: double and single thread. Single thread is the most adaptable as double thread may distort some stitches. Canvas comes in several widths and is defined by the number of threads to the inch. Popular sizes are 14, 16 or 18 threads to 1 inch (2.5 cm). Cotton canvas is suitable for panels and small items but linen canvas wears better for items such as chair seats. Rug canvas is suitable for large-scale work.
Threads Tapestry and crewel wools are the traditional yarns and they are best for upholstery and items in constant use. Otherwise a variety of yarns can add interest to the work; examples include carpet thrums, silks, linen threads, stranded cottons, soft embroidery, pearl cottons and knitting yarns. If a thread does not cover the canvas, more than one strand can be used.
Needles Tapestry needles are used as they have round points and do not split canvas threads or yarn.
Frames and transferring designs Always use a slate frame and transfer the design by tracing through.

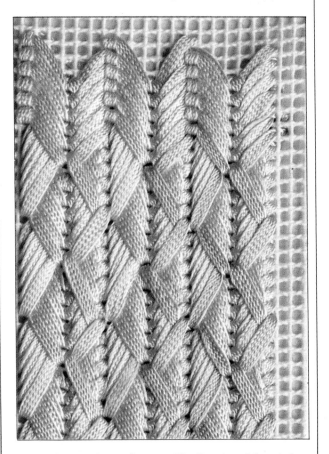

ABOVE: *An experimental sample using single canvas and multi-dyed rayon braid.*

The direction of the stitches and shaded thread give added interest.

PATTERN IN CANVASWORK

Trace out the main details of a sketch, photograph or a picture from a magazine. Transfer this design to the canvas. Select your threads to a limited colour scheme but choose a variety of thread weights and textures. Make a series of small samples in canvas-work stitches. Use them to practice working the stitches rhythmically and to an even tension and keep them as reference material for textures and patterns. You should include experiments with both single and double canvas. Vary the scale of the stitches to give an impression of perspective; small stitches for the background and larger ones in the foreground. Two or more stitches can be combined in innumerable ways to give other effects — even the angle at which the light falls on the stitches can be exploited. Shapes and strips of leather, suede or velvet can be applied.

In this example areas of painted canvas can be seen behind the long tramming stitches and illustrates the way in which rice stitch worked in two colours immediately gives a variety of pattern.

Horizontal tent stitch is one of the smallest canvaswork stitches — useful for fine detail, lines or for filling background areas. Because both sides are covered equally well, it is hardwearing and ideal for upholstery. Working from right to left, make a diagonal stitch upwards over one intersection, bring needle out to left of starting point (**1**). Complete row, insert needle above (**2**), turn work and repeat the sequence to finish (**3**).

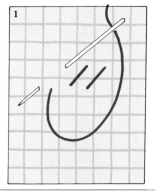

Vertical tent stitch: working downwards, bring needle out and make a diagonal stitch upwards over one inter-section. Pass needle diagonally behind and bring out below starting point (**1**). Finish the row, and take the needle to the back (**2**). Turn the work around and repeat the same sequence over the next row keeping an even tension throughout (**3**).

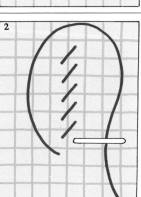
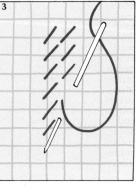

Diagonal tent stitch: working from top left to bottom right, bring needle out and make a diagonal stitch upwards over one intersection. Pass needle vertically behind and bring out two threads below (**1**). Complete the row, pass needle diagonally behind and bring out two threads down and one to left (**2**). Working upwards, make diagonal stitch over one intersection, pass needle behind and bring out two threads to left (**3**).

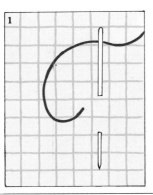  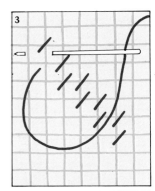

Long armed cross stitch gives an interesting plaited effect — useful for borders and infilling. Make a diagonal stitch upwards over two threads and four threads to right. Pass needle behind and bring out two threads to left (**1**). Make a diagonal stitch downwards over two threads and two to right. Pass needle behind and bring out two threads to left (**2**). Repeat the sequence to end of row (**3**).

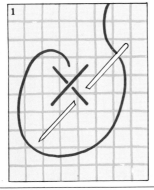 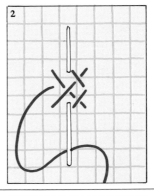 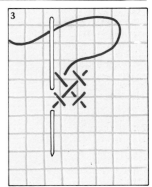

Rice stitch covers the canvas well and gives a dense, rough texture. Working from right to left, make a cross stitch over two intersections. Bring needle out at centre top. Insert at centre right and bring out at centre bottom (**1**). Reinsert at centre right and bring out at centre left. Work the other corners in the same way (**2**). Complete the cross and bring needle out two threads below, ready to make the next stitch (**3**).

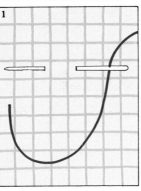 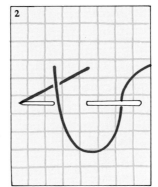 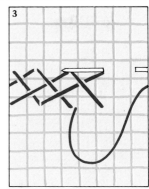

Smyrna stitch, or double cross stitch, gives a raised, knubbly texture. Make a cross stitch over four intersections and bring needle out at centre bottom. Insert needle at centre top and bring out at centre left (**1**). Insert needle at centre right to complete the stitch, and bring out four threads across and two down. Repeat the sequence over four intersections (**2**). Work subsequent rows in opposite direction (**3**).

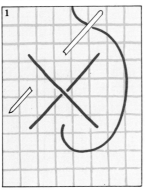 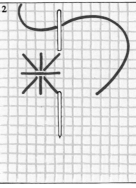 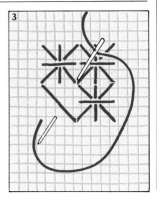

CROSS STITCH

Cross stitch is probably one of the oldest forms of embroidery. It is used all over the world, particularly in peasant communities. The stitch is made in two stages with two diagonals worked over each other to form a cross. It is usually worked on canvas or evenweave fabric. When working on canvas the stitches should cover the ground completely, while on linen or similar fabric the crosses form a pattern on the surface. Sometimes cross stitch is worked on a fabric whose threads are not easily countable, for example velvet. In this case tack a canvas or net of suitable mesh onto the fabric to be worked and work the cross stitching through both layers without piercing the threads of the canvas or net. When the embroidery is complete the strands of the overlaid material are pulled away without disturbing the stitches. Cross stitches must cross in the same direction.

BELOW: Poppies — *a modern example of free cross stitch, of varying weight of thread, size and diection of stitch.*

RIGHT: *Detail of a Central European shirt, stitched in closely worked cross stitch on an evenweave cloth.*

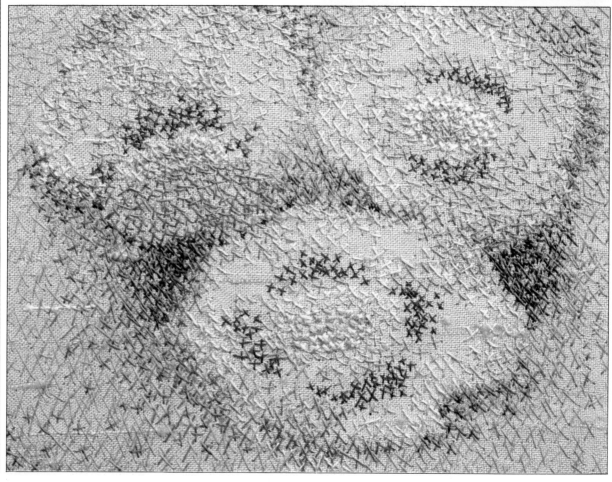

Assisi embroidery
This type of embroidery originated in Assisi, Italy; it is a variation on cross stitch. Its main characteristic is that the design is reversed, with the background stitched and the motifs left unfilled or voided.

Long-armed cross stitch (or plaited Slav stitch) was originally used, but modern interpretations use simple cross stitch. The work is started by outlining the design with back or double-running (Holbein) stitch. All the outline stitches must lie vertically or horizontally, so that the entire fabric between the motifs is covered.

Plan the design on graph paper, and choose an evenweave fabric whose threads can be easily counted.

LEFT: *A stitch detail from an early example of Assisi work, using back stitch and long-armed cross.*

Italian cross stitch is completely reversible — useful for tablelinen. Working over three threads and three intersections, begin by making a horizontal back stitch. Then make a diagonal stitch bringing needle out at starting point (**1**). Make an upright stitch and pass needle diagonally behind, ready to make the next stitch (**2**). Work the next and subsequent rows above to complete stitches in previous row (**3**).

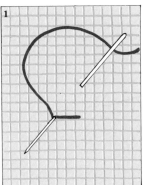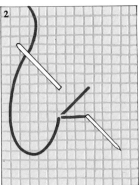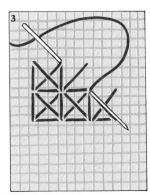

Montenegrin stitch: make a diagonal stitch two threads up and six threads to right. Pass needle diagonally behind and bring out three threads to left and two down (**1**). Make a short diagonal stitch up to left, insert needle two threads above starting point. Bring out where thread last emerged (**2**). Make an upright stitch over two threads, bring out at same point and repeat sequence (**3**).

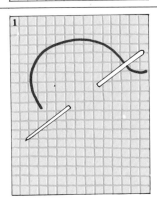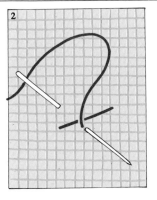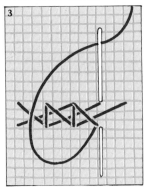

PULLED WORK

Pulled work is another name for drawn fabric work; the former name helps avoid the confusion between drawn thread and drawn fabric work. In pulled work, the threads of the fabric are pulled or drawn together to make lacy patterns, whereas in drawn thread work threads are actually withdrawn from the fabric.

Pulled work has always been popular in Britain, particularly during the eighteenth century, when it was used on coverlets and gentlemen's waistcoats. These were sometimes quilted to give extra warmth. Traditionally, it was worked in self-colour, relying on contrasting areas of texture produced by the stitches to give the work its character. However, there is no reason not to experiment with colour in pulled work.

The method is used mainly for functional purposes, and is still used a great deal for tablelinen of all kinds. An evenweave fabric, on which the threads can be easily counted, should be chosen. Linen, which launders well,

is excellent for household articles, but you may experiment with many dress and furnishing fabrics which, provided they are not too tightly woven, will pull into the lacy patterns. Scrim is a very good fabric to experiment with; it looks well in its natural colour, and also dyes well.

The stitching thread must be strong, as there is a considerable strain on each stitch. It should be about the same weight as the threads of the background fabric, but experiment with thicker and thinner threads to see the difference in effect. Heavier threads will give greater contrast, especially when working stitches in the satin stitch group. Linen threads, if available, are good, but fine coton perlé or crochet cotton can also be used. Use a fine tapestry needle, which will separate the fabric threads without splitting them. Take care to get the correct tension; if working in a frame, do not stretch the fabric too tightly.

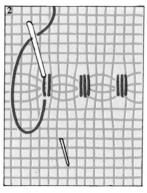

LEFT: *In this detail of a Persian cover, the use of stitched geometrical patterns in contrast with a filigree of pulled holes exploits the way in which the light falls on a complex surface.*

ABOVE: *This patterned border of a Turkish towel, relies on colour for its design and is typical of Turkish embroidery; although called towels, such pieces were used as covering cloths.*

Coil filling stitch: working from right to left, make three straight stitches upwards over three threads. Pull thread firmly, pass needle diagonally behind four inter- sections and bring out (**1**). Repeat to end of row and bring needle out four threads down and two to right (**2**). Repeat stitch sequence, working from left to right (**3**), and continue in this way to fill area.

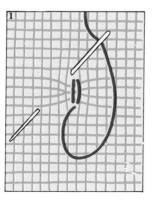

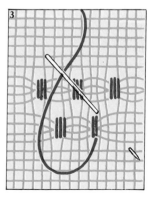

ABOVE: *A detail of eighteenth-century whitework, showing pulled work fillings. The numerous openwork patterns which decorate the stylized flower shapes are enclosed by closely worked satin and buttonhole stitch.*

EXPERIMENTAL PULLED WORK

Owing to the limitations of the technique, pulled work will always tend to be fairly regular. Use traditional stitches on a variety of fabrics: linen, hessian, scrim, open furnishing fabrics.

This modern example worked on loosely woven scrim, makes full use of the contrast between the thread and the spaces created by pulling the background fabric.

Four-sided stitch is worked from right to left over four threads and four inter-sections. Make an upright straight stitch and bring needle out four threads to left (**1**). Insert needle at starting point, pass it diagonally behind four inter-sections and bring out (**2**). Work the same stitch in reverse (**3**). Remember at each stage of making the stitch to pull the working thread firmly. Work the next stitch by repeating the last three stages (**4**). At the end of the row bring the needle out after completing a stitch (**5**) and then turn the work around ready to embroider the next row above (**6**).

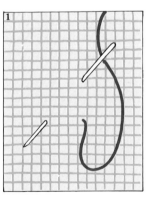

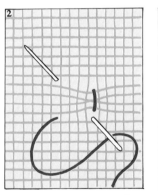

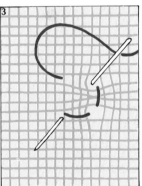

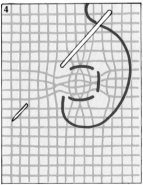

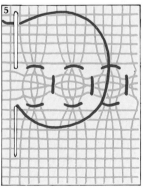

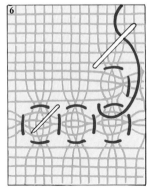

PATTERN DARNING

Pattern darning, as its name implies, is darning used as embroidery. It is worked in parallel rows of straight stitches, in varying lengths, so as to form a pattern on the surface of the background fabric. This should be of an even weave, or at least have easily countable threads, as the regularity of the stitching is of the utmost importance for this method.

The straight stitches are derived from those used for quite utilitarian purposes; the origin of darning is 'making good' a worn surface by reinforcement using suitable threads. Many rows of running stitch worked evenly, to resemble weaving, become a darning stitch, used to repair weak patches in clothing and household linen. In embroidery, darning and running stitch are almost the same, the difference being that the latter may be the same length under the fabric as on top, and it can be used in single rows.

Pattern darning, however, can be more decorative. Straight stitches are worked so that the stitching thread is interrupted on the surface by a thread (or threads) of the background fabric, where the needle dips below the surface. In this way, you are forming a pattern by making use of the weave.

You can make many beautiful and simple designs by varying the colours used. Stitches can be arranged to form various designs; the most common is the over-all diaper pattern. Its simplicity has made pattern darning popular throughout the world from earliest times; it has been used most effectively on peasant garments, and on samplers to extend and embellish hand-woven fabrics. Many of these patterns cover large areas and appear to form an integral part of the cloth.

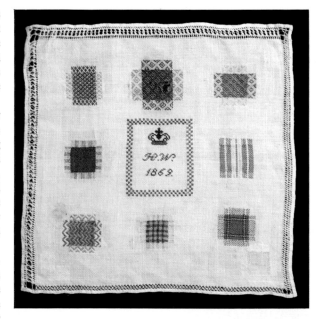

ABOVE: *Developments of the basic darning stitch can be seen in this nineteenth-century German sampler. The patterns simulate those created in intricately woven cloth, and are extended by the use of contrasting colour (as seen in the detail, RIGHT) worked along the warp and weft of the evenweave fabric. Samplers have been used as a source of reference for many centuries.*

LEFT: *Darning stitches, worked closely together, form an all-over pattern on this corner of a Caucasian cover. The density of stitches gives the appearance of a woven fabric, rather than embroidery. The change of direction of the lines of stitching exploits the play of light on the surface of smooth, silky threads. The subtle interplay of colour between the blue background fabric and the browns and blues of the thread enriches the surface still further.*

Covers were used for many purposes, which might include covering a bed or a chest.

ABOVE: *A modern example of the use of darning to hold down layers of semi-transparent fabric. The contrasting rows of blue and yellow running stitch integrate the fabric, but do not rely on the weave to make an effect.*

LEFT: *The front opening on this Spanish shirt shows a very elaborate form of pattern darning. The intricate stitch, worked in black thread on white, adds richness to the plain fabric. Interesting patterns are built up, some almost solid and others open, resembling black lace.*

DRAWN THREAD

Drawn thread work is of peasant origin. In the nineteenth and early twentieth centuries, a great deal of drawn thread work was done, mainly for household linen; because modern methods of laundering are unsuitable for delicate work it is now less popular for such articles.

Any strong fabric from which threads can easily be drawn is suitable. Experiment with loosely woven furnishing fabrics and unusual threads. If the work is intended for tablelinen, an even weave linen is the best choice. The threads are withdrawn from the fabric horizontally or vertically, and the remaining threads are decorated and strengthened by binding and additional stitches.

As the threads are withdrawn from an evenly woven fabric, designs are based on straight lines or rectangular shapes, which should not be too large; if too many threads are withdrawn from one place the fabric is considerably weakened. Design the whole area in blocks of tone — the darkest blocks representing areas which will have the most threads removed. Working with cut paper is a good design method for this technique, as squares and rectangles of paper can be moved around easily.

In the simplest form of drawn thread work the threads are withdrawn in one direction only and neatened with decorative hemstitching. This method is traditionally used for finishing the hems on evenweave fabric.

Withdrawn threads: in order to work decorative drawn thread borders, certain threads have first to be removed from the ground fabric. Withdraw sufficient threads for the depth of the border required. Do this starting in the middle and working outwards towards the end of the border. With a pin, lift one thread in the middle and cut through using embroidery scissors. Withdraw the thread on both sides back to the end of the border, leaving ends long enough to thread into a needle (**1**). Neaten the edges of the border on the wrong side weaving the ends back into the main fabric for about ¾ in (2cm) (**2**). Neaten the opposite end of border ready for working the hemstitching.

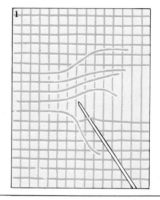
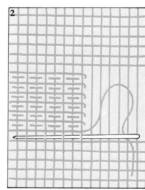

Hemstitch can be worked on single fabric, without a hem, from the wrong side. Begin by running the thread into the bottom left corner leaving a 4in (10cm) length of thread. Make a single stitch over the first thread. Pass needle behind three threads, (**1**). Bring needle out, pass it behind two horizontal threads and bring through, pulling firmly (**2**). Neaten threads through hem stitching on wrong side.

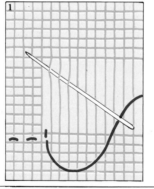
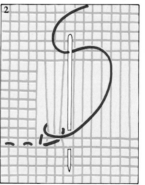
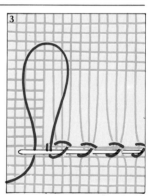

Simple twist: make from the right side on evenly hem-stitched border. Secure working thread to edge of fabric. Place needle behind second group of threads with needle tip on first group (**1**). Press needle tip on first group and slip it behind twisting the first group to left of second (**2**). Pull needle through keeping thread tight and twisted threads in place. Complete the border (**3**).

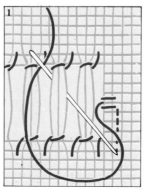
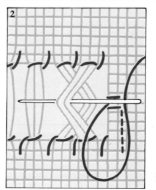
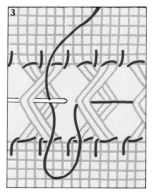

ABOVE: *The delicacy of drawn thread work on fine fabric is evident in this charming mat. The open work of the* whipped and twisted loose threads contrasts with the plain border and fringe.

ABOVE: *Detail of a sleeve and underarm gusset, showing how the seams joining the pieces have been decorated to become a feature of the garment. Additional emphasis is given by bands of needleweaving and stitching which follow the lines of the seams.*

In needleweaving, groups of parallel threads are whipped together to form patterns.

ABOVE: *Modern Hardanger originated in Norway. Blocks of satin stitch — Kloster blocks — are worked around shapes, before the threads are cut and withdrawn. Each block consists of an uneven number of stitches, and encloses an even number of threads. Only the threads which lie in the same direction are cut; the rest are decorated with overcasting and interweaving. The spaces are sometimes filled with additional loops* and picots. The geometric blocks have been used to build this motif.

LEFT: *Russian drawn thread work is usually set in a square or rectangle, in this case surrounded by a border and decorative hem. The edge is secured by overcasting or close buttonhole stitch, then some background threads are removed horizontally and vertically. The remaining lattice is overcast diagonally across the fabric, with two stitches to each bar and one or two to each intersection.*

ALTERING THE SURFACE
CUTWORK

Cutwork is a type of embroidery in which the parts of the background fabric are cut away to emphasize the design. There are several types. In *simple cutwork*, the outlines are embroidered in buttonhole stitch, and some of the shapes cut away. *Renaissance work* is more elaborate; the cut-away areas are larger, and are decorated with 'brides' or 'bars'. Still more elaborate is *Richelieu work*; the bars are embellished with 'picots', producing a lacy effect.

More intricate forms of cutwork, which are Italian in origin, include *reticella*, where large areas of the background are cut away, and the spaces filled with needlelace patterns.

For renaissance and Richelieu work, work the bars at the same time as the running stitches, before the buttonhole stitches are worked and the background fabric cut away. Carry the working thread across the design, at the point where the bar is to be worked. Make a tiny holding stitch, and take the thread back across the space. Make a second holding stitch, and return the thread once more, so that the bar consists of three threads. These must be pulled fairly taut. Anchor the thread firmly.

The bar must now be covered closely in buttonhole stitches, which are kept quite detached from the background fabric. Continue outlining the shapes in running stitch, working all the bars. When this step is complete, the outline buttonhole stitches can be worked as before. When cutting away the background spaces, take care not to cut the bars.

To work picots, buttonhole to the centre of the bar and insert a pin into the bar and the background fabric, at right angles to the bar. Loop the working thread under the pin, without piercing the fabric, then up over the bar and out underneath. Slip the needle under the loop and over the bar, and twist the thread around the needle before pulling it through. Pull the thread tight and remove the pin.

MATERIALS

It is essential to use a closely woven background fabric, otherwise the cut-away edges are liable to fray. If the embroidery is to be purely decorative, and thus will not require constant washing or handling, then light-weight iron-on interfacing can be applied to the wrong side. Traditional cut work uses self-coloured embroidery thread, and relies on the cut areas to give the design its character. If coloured threads are used, great care should be taken that they do not overpower the design. A pair of sharp-pointed embroidery scissors is an essential tool.

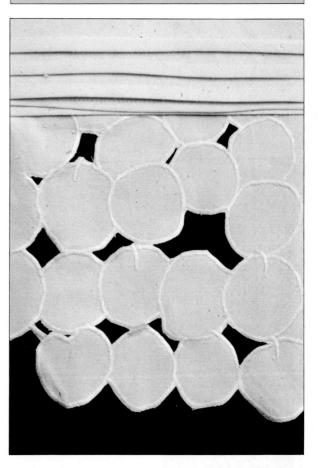

ABOVE: *This sachet cover shows skilled use of cutwork. The figures and trees are left, and the background cut away. A tracery of bars provides a frame.*

ABOVE: *Working cutwork by hand is a laborious process, and it is worthwhile considering the use of a swing-needle sewing machine. Rows of machine satin stitch instead of buttonhole stitch can be very effective. Machine stitching is just as strong as hand stitchery, and has the advantage that the fabric can be cut away on both sides of the stitching. Experiment with scrap fabrics and your own sewing machine. It is often helpful to put a sheet of tissue paper or other thin paper underneath the fabric when you are machining. This can be torn away afterwards.*

RIGHT: *A detail of seventeenth-century cutwork. The fine background fabric is handspun, handwoven linen. The delicate, intricate pattern made by the cut spaces is further embellished with whipping stitches and needle-woven fillings. A narrow band of lace, decorated with picots, is used to finish the edge of the border. Such fine detailed work is similar to needlemade lace.*

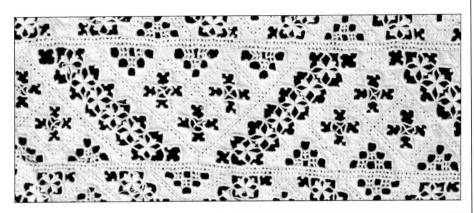

EXPLORING SIMPLE CUTWORK

Select a spray of flowers and make outline drawings with simple repeating shapes suitable for cut work. Cut out the design in white paper, and stick it down on black, so that the areas to be cut away stand out clearly. Transfer the design to the background fabric. Work two close parallel rows of running stitch round each motif, to act as padding; then work closely-spaced buttonhole stitches to cover the double lines of running stitch. The looped edges of the buttonhole stitches must face the part of the design that is to be cut away. When the stitchery is complete, carefully cut away the spaces, as close as possible to the stitches. Alternatively, a design like this can be worked on the machine.

Experiment with several layers of transparent fabrics. Work your design on the sewing machine, then cut away to reveal different fabrics in different sections.

Experiment with colour. Use a combination of fabric paints and machine stitchery to build up a landscape for panels; or use coloured threads and fabrics for hand work.

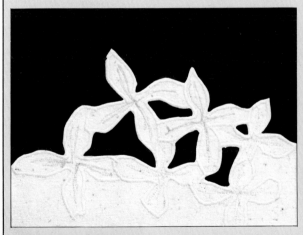

Simplified overlapping petals traced from a drawing of flowers were the inspiration for this waistcoat border. Cut areas between the petals to form a pretty, delicate edging.

PLEATS, TUCKS AND FOLDS

The manipulation of fabric into pleats, tucks and folds has both a practical and a decorative purpose. Many inspiring examples can be found in historical costume. Ancient Egyptians wore garments of the finest linen, very transparent and often pleated in a sun-ray pattern. In Greece during the first Ionic period, men and women wore clothes fluted with pleats and tucks. In the seventeenth century there was a fashion for ruffs, which circled the neck from collar to chin. The round shape was obtained by using several layers of fine linen one over the other, each pleated like a fan.

In more recent years fine pleating has been used by fashion designers to create elegant flowing dresses reminiscent of those worn in Ancient Greece.

Fabrics

Linens, cottons, silks, woollens and synthetics all have their special characteristics, and will behave in different ways when pleated, tucked and folded. For instance, some synthetics are crease-resistant and therefore difficult to pleat. Tucking is most effective on fine fabrics such as cotton lawn or pure silk. Most fabrics will fold well even if too springy to pleat or tuck successfully.

Pleats

Pleats are even folds, usually having rigid sharp edges, and can be set and secured in a variety of ways. They reduce the width of the fabric evenly and regularly. The spaces between the pleats as well as their depth can give a variety of pattern and contrast of surface and shadow. Functional pleats are usually fixed at one end only, but many decorative effects can be achieved by stitching them at both ends. Sections worked in this way can be incorporated into garments. The texture and weight of the fabric used will affect the appearance of the pleats; for example velvet will give a rich opulent look.

ABOVE: *In this detail of an apron from the Balearic Islands, pleats are tightly* *drawn together and covered with a variety of embroidery stitches.*

Tucks

Fine pin-tucking is often used on garments to ensure a good fit, but it can also become part of the decoration, sometimes further enhanced with insertions of lace. On more experimental work the tucks can be made both vertically and horizontally, building up into a grid pattern. Beads, buttons, laces, ribbons and embroidery can be added to enrich the surface. The size of the tucks can be varied from very narrow to wider; some can be folded back at intervals and secured with embroidery. They can be used together with pleats and folds, which will give even greater change of scale and complexity.

Folds

A gathering thread of running stitches can be drawn up to bunch the fabric into folds, evenly or unevenly. Patterns can be created by drawing up fabric at regularly spaced intervals and securing them with stitches. The play of light on the surface will vary according to the texture of the fabric; tonal effects and even the illusion of movement can be created in this way. Silk, velvet, chiffon and lace will all fall into graceful folds.

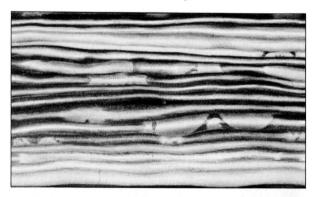

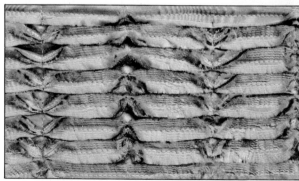

ABOVE: *A drawing of folded Indian printed silk, translated by machining several layers of muslin into tucks. By cutting these in places and machining* *asymmetrically through them, the frayed edges of different colours are opened out and held securely into position.*

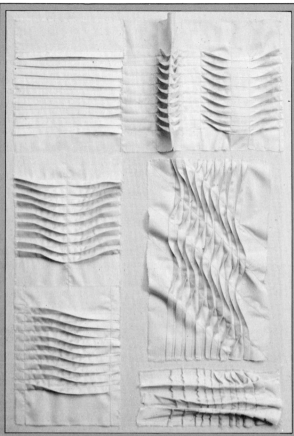

LEFT: *These tucks are made by running a line of machine stitching parallel to the fold in series. This basically very simple use of stitches alters the fabric surface. The depth and interval between the pleats affects the depth of surface and shadows. Additional machining running vertically up and down or diagonally across the first horizontal set will give more complex variations, and the play of light will be broken up further. Tonal effects, and even illusions of movement can be created in this way. The tension built up by many lines of stitches will tend to twist the fabric, suggesting three-dimensional forms.*

Sequences that explore small to large, varying intervals and proportions, complex to plain areas, straight and twisted forms will provide a wealth of visual effects. Grids, systems and sequences can be set up and extended by the addition or subtraction of colour and pattern, beads, laces, braids and ribbons, or areas of embroidery.

The textures and patterns of the fabrics themselves, from the weave, knit, or a printed design, may be distorted and rearranged by pleating, folding and tucking. The rigidity or looseness of a fabric, its patterning, its degree of transparency and the way in which it absorbs or reflects light affect the character of each surface; any change of fabric, thread, stitch or spacing will alter the effect.

RIGHT: *1 A gathering thread of random running stitch has been drawn up to bunch stockinette into uneven folds. 2 A formal pattern has been made by drawing fabric together into folds at regularly spaced intervals. 3 A circle of patterned fabric has been applied to another. The fullness created by drawing up a gathering thread worked round the edge has been set into folds with stab stitches.*

What happens if these experimental pieces are stretched or twisted? Will they tie together to form a structure, or link to form a hanging? How far can the idea be scaled up in size?

Look at the fabric piece from all sorts of angles, with different kinds and positions of lighting, perhaps with convex or concave reflective surfaces; consider its frayed or cut edges, the tensions created, the way the patterns and textures respond. Taking photographs of different shapes can be an interesting way of extending ideas.

Pleat patterned or striped fabrics to obscure and distort the design. If stripes are pleated together, it gives the appearance of solid colour; when the fullness is released the complete pattern will be apparent. This can be particularly effective on a garment; use it to make an enriched form of pleating over the shoulders, round the waist, or at the wrist.

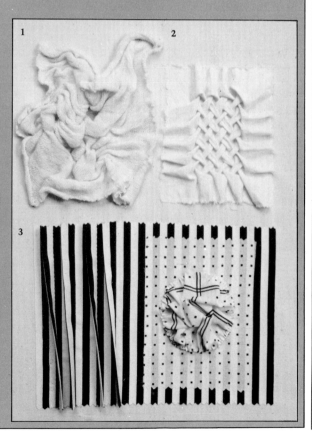

SMOCKING

Smocking could be described as an elaborate and decorative form of pleating. It evolved as gathering held in place by rows of stitches worked over the pleats, very regularly and evenly. Traditionally it was often worked on linen with self-coloured linen thread, to control fullness and allow stretch across the back and chest, and to shape the sleeves of landworkers' smocks. A wealth of diamond, rope, and wave patterns developed from a combination of four simple stitches — stem or rope, cable or basket, vandyke and chevron. A further two stitches, honeycomb and feather, were later additions. The beauty of smocking relies on the way in which the various stitches arrange the pleats into different groupings and directions; how spaced at intervals and in varying proportions, decorative bands and units of pattern are created. The fretwork of pleats remaining unstitched is as important to the elasticity, tonal effects, textures and patterns of smocking as the embroidery itself.

The complexity of the embroidered designs reached a peak in the middle years of the nineteenth century, and included boxes of complementary patterns worked in single, double, treble feather stitch and eyelet holes, stem and chain stitches. These were worked both for decorative effect and to strengthen the places most subject to wear. Pleated and embroidered epaulettes over the shoulders also gave extra protection from rain and the rub of yokes.

Versions of the landworker's smock and smocking are to be found throughout the world and vary in decorative detail and function.

ABOVE: *A detail of a smocked sleeve with smocking at the wrist, a decorative panel and cuff edging in single feather stitch, and traditional Dorset wheel buttons.*

LEFT: *A woman's bonnet of unbleached cotton shaped by a narrow band of smocking in bright colours, surrounded by rich embroidered patterns and bobbin lace.*

ABOVE: *A smock made for and exhibited at the Great Exhibition in London in 1851. It is delicately worked, with panels of* *feather stitch and leaf motifs worked into the collar and shoulders.*

There have been several revivals of interest in the traditional smock (for instance, by some of the followers of William Morris) in reaction to the goods and values of industrialization. More recently fashion designers, particularly designers of children's clothes, have made many decorative and effective innovations in smocking by selecting and combining different fabrics, methods and styles and by using coloured fabrics and threads.

Technique

Any fabric which will gather easily is suitable. The width of the fabric required depends on the type of fabric, the distance between the pleats and the tension of the stitches. As a general rule allow three times the width of the finished piece but test this by working a small amount of smocking on a measured piece. The fabric is tacked across in rows on the wrong side and drawn up into even pleats with the tacking threads which are then tied securely.

Work along each row. On the completion of a row, unthread the needle and leave the thread loose. Tack the required number of rows, then draw up the pleats by

holding the loose ends of the threads in pairs, carefully easing each row along its gathering thread until the right width and distribution is settled. Secure the ends around pins or knot them in pairs.

Any kind of thread is suitable for smocking, providing it pulls through the fabric easily and does not snap. Make sure you have enough thread to complete each line. Secure the embroidery thread on the wrong side with a knot, or a double stitch into the back of a pleat. On the right side, work the smocking stitches, regularly and with even tension, by picking up a small portion of the top edges of the pleats. Put the last stitch through to the wrong side and fasten off into the back of the last pleat. When complete, draw out the gathering threads.

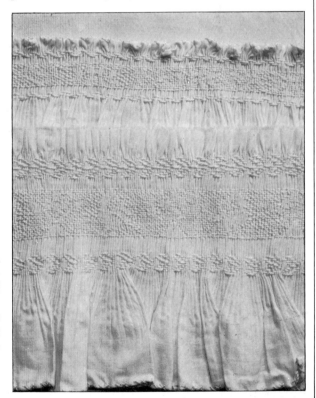

ABOVE AND RIGHT: *A variation of smocking from Mexico, in which the stitches run through the pleats, rather than whipping over them, to build up blocks and voided image-based patterns.*

Tacking and gathering: begin with a knot and working on the wrong side, from right to left, work rows of gathering stitches picking up the fabric between the dots. Leave ends of threads hanging loose at left side (**1**). Pull up the threads evenly so that they are not too tight (**2**). Even out the folds and tie the threads in pairs at the left side (**3**).

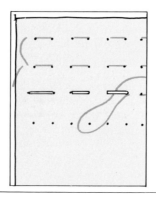 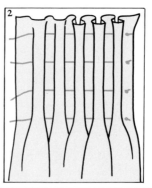 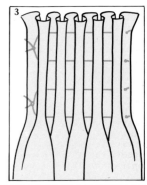

Honeycomb stitch: working from left to right, bring needle out on first line and back stitch first and second folds together with thread below needle (**1**). Repeat, and slip the needle through fold to emerge inside second fold on line below (**2**). Back stitch second and third folds together (**3**). Repeat, and slip needle upwards through fold to emerge inside third fold on line above (**4**). Continue working alternately up and down to row end *(see bottom right)*.

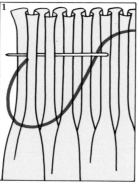 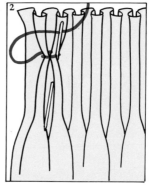 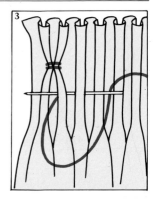

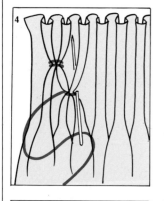

Surface honeycomb stitch is worked in a similar way to honeycomb stitch but has the working thread on the surface. Working from left to right, back stitch second fold with thread above needle (**1**). Pull thread firmly, and back stitch second fold on row below (**2**). With thread below needle, back stitch third fold (**3**). Pull thread tight, and back stitch third fold above (**4**). Repeat sequence. Continue to end of row *(see bottom right)*.

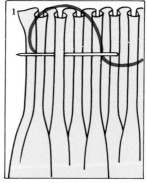

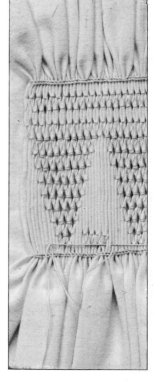

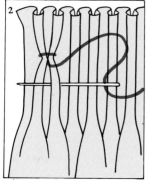 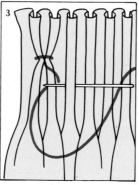 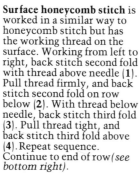 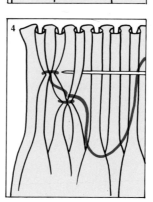

Cable stitch (below) is a firm control stitch. Working from left to right, bring needle up through first fold, and with thread below needle, back stitch the second fold, pulling thread firmly (**1**). With thread below needle, back stitch third fold (**2**). Continue to work with thread alternately above and below needle to row end (**3**). Rows may be worked close together or spaced apart (*see top right*).

Stem stitch (right) is a firm control stitch often used to enclose more elastic stitches. Bring needle out through first fold, back stitch the second fold with the thread below needle. Continue in this way to end of row. To slant the stem stitch in the opposite direction, work with the thread above the needle. The two rows may be worked close together or at either side of a border (*see top right*).

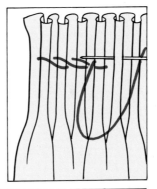

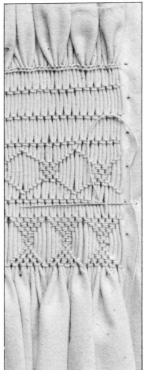

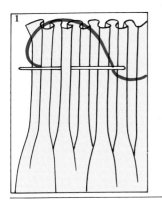

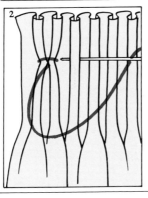

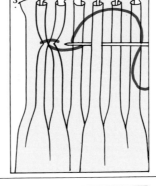

Chevron stitch is a very elastic stitch. Working from left to right, bring needle out on second row down. Back stitch second fold with thread below needle (**1**). Pull thread, back stitch second fold on first row (**2**). With thread above needle, back stitch third fold (**3**). Pull thread, back stitch fold on second row (**4**). Repeat sequence to row end and work following rows below (*see bottom right*).

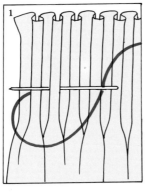

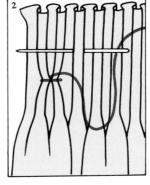

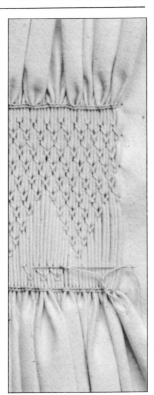

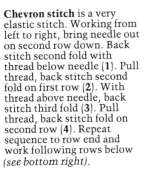

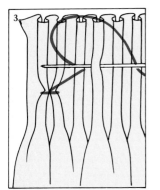

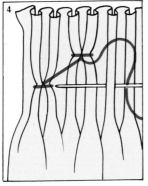

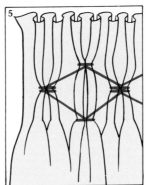

Vandyke stitch: working from right to left, back stitch first and second folds together with thread above needle (**1**). Take needle to second row and back stitch second and third folds together (**2**). With thread below needle, make a second back stitch (**3**). Stitch third and fourth folds together on first row (**4**). Repeat the sequence to row end and work next and following rows below (**5**) *(see top right)*.

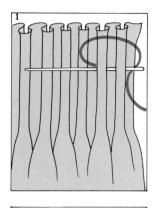

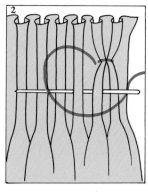

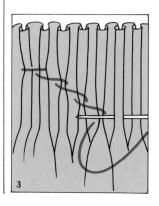

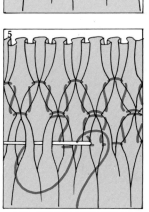

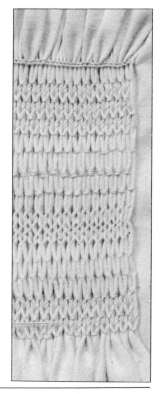

Wave stitch is a fairly firm control stitch. Working from left to right and with thread above needle, back stitch second fold (**1**) and then the third fold below (**2**). Working diagonally downwards, back stitch the fourth and fifth folds. With thread below needle, back stitch sixth fold across ready to work upwards (**3**). Work sequence in reverse (**4**) and repeat to row end (**5**) *(see bottom right)*.

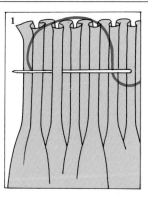

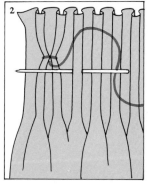

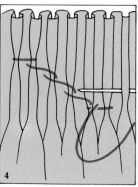

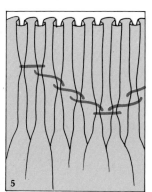

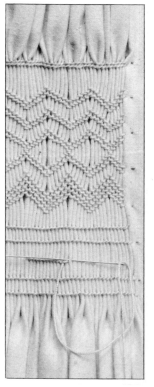

FREE EXPERIMENTAL SMOCKING

Consider how a patterned or textured fabric can be affected by smocking. Alter the background by withdrawing threads, by dyeing, painting or printing.

Instead of keeping the tacking stitches evenly spaced, work them at random, in different sizes and directions.

Leave unpleated spaces parallel to the drawn-up columns of pleats, perhaps in different widths and varying intervals. These spaces could be left blank or filled with embroidery, insertions of lace, braid or ribbon.

Try leaving the tacking threads in and making them a feature. The threads could be in different colours and weights.

When choosing the threads consider their various qualities. Matching the threads to the fabric will enhance the texture. The play of light on shiny threads will give added contrast and interest, and working with colour will give interesting effects.

Some of the exciting possibilities available when exploring free experimental smocking are shown on the study sheet below. The use of colour can give dramatic or subtle variations to the basic technique.

QUILTING

Quilting, derived from the Latin word *culcita* meaning a mattress or pillow, is a means of stitching several layers of fabric together which has been used for warmth over a long period by many cultures. The technique has also been used for protective garments in times of war, on its own or under chainmail or plate armour.

Examples of corded quilting have survived from the sixteenth century, and from the late seventeenth century there are examples of quilts, hangings and headwear which are closely covered with corded quilting. From approximately the beginning of the eighteenth century, wadded quilting was used for patchwork covers to produce the familiar patchwork quilts. The early settlers in America took patchwork and quilting traditions across the Atlantic; their patchwork used good cloth from worn clothing and was quilted for warmth. In the nineteenth century corded quilting was used with whalebone to stiffen the fabric in stays, creating lovely patterns. In Britain, there are regional traditions of quilting in Durham, Cumberland, Northumberland, Westmorland, Wales and south-west England.

The simplest quilting was based on diagonal lines making squares, but many designs were very intricate and templates — ready-cut, shaped elements of the pattern — were used in such cases to mark out the design. The quilting would be done with the work on a frame.

Shadow quilting

This is a variation of corded and stuffed quilting. A semi-transparent fabric such as fine silk, organdie or voile is used on top. Muslin is used as a backing and brightly coloured yarns as the filling. The yarn colours are muted by the top fabric, creating subtle effects.

BELOW: *A repeat pattern of trees, in shadow quilting. Some shapes are filled with flat pieces of coloured felt,* *inserted from the back, others are stuffed with coloured fabrics to give a more rounded surface.*

MATERIALS

Fabrics Smooth natural fibre fabrics work best; cotton, silk, fine wool, cotton/wool mixture, some polyester cottons, some synthetic satins and crêpes which are soft to *handle, single-weight* jersey fabrics, fine leather and suede.
Threads It is usual to match the fibre of the sewing thread to that of the top fabric, particularly where the item is to be washed frequently. A wide range of sewing threads is available, including a buttonhole twist for heavier stitching. Embroidery threads can be used where suitable. There is also a quilting thread which is especially strong, but its colour range and availability are limited.

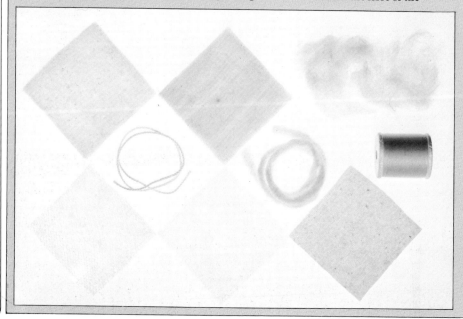

A selection of materials used for quilting showing, from left to right on the top row: the traditional woollen wadding known as domette; polyester wadding; and cotton domette. The middle row shows: the twisted cord used for corded quilting; soft quilting wool and a reel of quilting thread. On the bottom row: polyester wadding covered with a skin; cotton wadding covered with a skin; and loose polyester filling.

ABOVE: *A Chinese Turkestan cap of red silk. The main part is worked in corded quilting. Each section is outlined with* buttonhole stitch. The lower border is a wide band of black cotton worked with red and white cotton thread.

Cord quilting: tack fabric to backing with traced design stitching in both directions (**1**). Stitch around double lines of design using small running stitches (**2**). With wrong side facing, snip into channel. Thread bodkin with quilting cord, pass through channel a little at a time, bringing needle out on curves or angles (**3**): reinsert leaving a little cord on surface (**4**).

BOTTOM RIGHT: *A quilted belt in heavy cream satin, based on a design of natural forms.*

Corded (Italian) quilting

Corded quilting can be worked using either one or two layers of fabric. (Originally fine linen and a linen scrim, were used as a backing fabric. Muslin may also be used as a backing fabric.) A firm smooth cotton cord is used as filling between parallel lines of stitching. 'Italian' quilting, which first appeared during the 1930s, uses a soft thick wool as the filling thread and gives a softer line.

The parallel lines of stitches are now usually worked in back stitch, or straight lines of machine-stitching. The channel between the two rows of stitching may be varied. Piping cord, which will give a slightly ridged effect, may be used. All cords must be shrunk before use to prevent the work puckering later.

There are two methods of working. The more versatile is the two-layer method. Stiffer cords can be worked with one layer of fabric. To do this press the fabric and mark the design by the chosen method, on the right side of the fabric. Frame up the fabric.

One hand holds the cord in place under the fabric. The other hand works herringbone stitch across the parallel lines of the design. This gives the appearance of two lines of back stitch on the right side and holds the cord in place as the work proceeds. Where lines cross each other cut the cord close to the stitching. Corded quilting is usually lined to prevent rubbing and to give a neat finish.

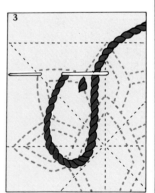

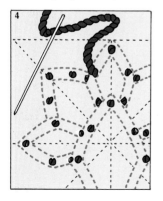

Stitches for quilting

The stitch most commonly used for traditional quilting is running stitch which gives a pleasing broken line. Where a more pronounced line is required back stitch may be used. Many other embroidery stitches may also be used particularly for wadded quilting. Chain stitch and Portuguese knotted stemstitch are most suitable, but it is worth experimenting with other line stitches for their decorative qualities. The stitch, however, should not be too dominant. Even stitching is more important than tiny stitches when using running stitch — an approximate guide for length is from ⅛-¼ in (3-6mm), depending on the thickness of the wadding used.

Quilting in a frame is recommended for large pieces of work. Assemble the layers and tack to hold (**1**). Place on backing fabric, right side up, allowing the end to hang free on far side. Tack through layers along nearest runner. Smooth fabric and pin layers on opposite runner (**2**). Do not pull fabrics too tight. Secure side edges of fabric to frame with tape pinned and laced around stretchers (**3**).

Wadded (English) quilting

Quilting for patchwork can echo the shapes ¼ in (6mm) from the seams or form a counterpoint to it (such as curved quilting with geometric shapes), with the design planned for the whole area.

Wadded quilting is composed of three layers — a top fabric which can be patchwork, appliqué or a single piece of fabric; a layer of wadding of appropriate thickness and texture; a backing layer of the same or slightly firmer weight than the top fabric so that the puffiness is thrown forward. Allow extra fabric and wadding to counteract the 'shrinkage' when quilting. In addition cut the backing fabric larger for attaching to the frame.

Wadding The traditional filling for domestic wadded quilting was either carded wool or cotton, which required close quilting to hold them in place. Cotton wadding is still obtainable; it has a skin on the outside and is used opened out with the fluffy side up.

Synthetic waddings are now available, including polyester wadding in several thicknesses. Triacetate wadding comes folded, with a skin like cotton wadding.

Assembly Place the backing layer right side down on a smooth surface, the centre wadding on top. Place the top fabric right side up on the wadding. Smooth the fabrics out from the centre and pin. Check that the backing is smooth, and tack in parallel lines from the centre to the

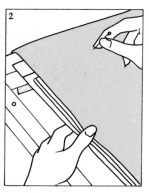

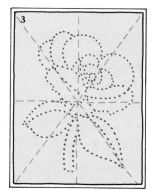

Trapunto quilting: transfer design to main fabric. Place backing and top fabric wrong sides together and tack in both directions (**1**). Outline the design with small running stitches (**2**). Working from the wrong side, snip the backing in the middle of each area to be padded (**3**). Using a round-ended bodkin, stuff the shape with teased out wadding (**4**). Mould each shape carefully and oversew the slits using matching sewing thread to finish (**5**).

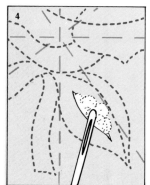

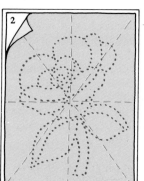

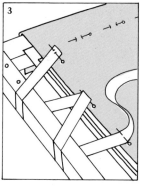

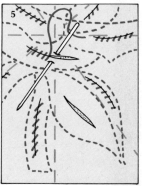

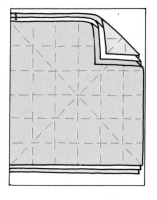

outside edges. Attach the work to the frame — a slightly looser tension is needed than that used for embroidery.

Stitching Using an up and down movement commence working from the centre of the piece outwards. This enables the work to be kept smooth.

Where the back of the work will not be seen, as in a quilt, begin with a small knot which is pulled through into the wadding. Finish stitching with a tiny backstitch, the needle splitting the last stitch. The end of the thread is run into the wadding before cutting off.

If the back of the work will not be visible, the stitching may be begun and ended with two tiny backstitches, running the thread into the wadding before cutting off.

Tied quilting. Mark top fabric with dots in grid formation, and pin or tack the three layers together. Thread needle with lengths of yarn and pick up fabrics below dot. Leave an end for tying and make a back stitch on top (1). Tie ends with reef knots. Trim or leave long, as preferred (2).

RIGHT: *A small purse with a decoration of tied quilting in silk threads.*

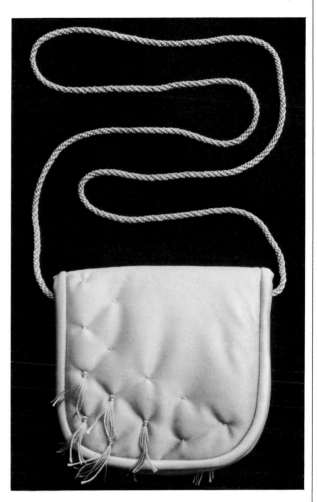

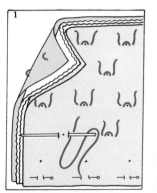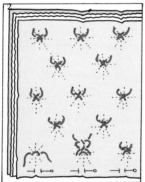

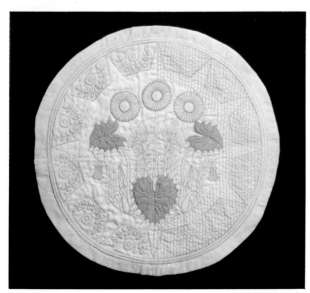

LEFT: *A 1930s cushion cover in shadow quilting. White organdie is laid over brightly coloured fabrics, giving the effect of muted pastel shades and a 'quilted' surface.*

Flat quilting

This method was very popular in the late seventeenth century. Two layers of fabric are used, the backing fabric being the same fibre but of a cheaper quality than the top fabric. The second layer gives the work more substance.

The design is transferred by the chosen method, the fabrics tacked together and held firmly in a frame. The design is worked in back stitch and when complete, the quilt is taken out of the frame and the tacking removed.

This method can also be worked by machine without a frame. The preparation of the fabrics is the same but the work is not framed up. Large pieces like quilts are cumbersome and must be rolled up, to allow the large quantity of fabric to pass under the arch of the main body of the machine. Smaller items, including garment pieces, are easy to handle in straight, zigzag or satin stitch.

STUMPWORK

Stumpwork, also known as raised work, reached the height of its popularity in the mid-seventeenth century. Its padded shapes and applied motifs give the work the appearance of a low relief carving. Although it is regarded as English, embroidery in relief was practised in many parts of Europe from the fourteenth century onwards, particularly in ecclesiastical decoration. English stumpwork, however, is a development of the raised and detached embroidery which first appeared in Elizabethan times, in which plaited gold stems were raised from the background, and petals or leaves were worked in detached button-hole stitch.

It is thought that stumpwork was mostly worked by young girls, who, after learning their stitches and techniques on samplers then went on to sew more decorative items. The subjects of the embroideries were usually scenes from the Bible or mythology. The figures were lavishly dressed in Stuart costume and set in elaborate landscapes. Trees, castles, animals, insects, flowers and fruits were added in profusion, with total disregard for scale. Occasionally fishponds would be included, complete with fish and a mermaid holding a tiny mirror which reflected her face.

Ivory coloured silk or satin was used for the background. Coloured wools, silks, metal threads, chenille, ribbons, spangles, beads and small pieces of mica were all used in the embroidery. Motifs, known as slips, were worked on fine canvas or linen, then carefully cut out and applied to the silk background. Shapes were padded with horsehair or lambswool, and then often covered with detached buttonhole stitch. Flower petals and leaves were usually worked in detached buttonhole stitch, sometimes over a wire framework so that they stood away from the background. Shaped wooden moulds were used for faces and hands; scraps of fabric and needlemade lace were used for canopies and clothes.

When the work was complete it would be mounted and framed as a picture, used as a frame for a mirror, or be sent to a cabinetmaker to be assembled into a casket. Some of the caskets were very elaborate, with hinged doors opening to reveal tiny drawers for holding needlework accessories. The similarity of the designs suggests that the background fabric was acquired by the embroideress ready prepared for working, together with the shaped wooden moulds.

This work shows great skill and ingenuity, and it is obvious that the young needlewomen must have enjoyed their tasks. Examples of their work can be found in both museums and private collections. Occasionally pieces have been left unfinished and provide an interesting source of study. Stumpwork has a charm of its own, but distance lends enchantment, and if slavishly copied now it would look too cluttered and fussy. However, by limiting the number of techniques in any one piece, and by using modern materials it can be attractive, interesting and fun to do. The designs should be kept simple and the colour schemes worked out carefully.

Techniques

Detached stitches such as buttonhole, hollie point and Ceylon are used extensively in stumpwork, and are particularly useful for covering padded shapes. Other stitches used are French knots, bullion knots, padded satin, seeding, rococo and couching.

Appliqué The shape to be applied should be cut slightly larger than the required finished size. Turn under the raw edges and secure in place with tiny slip stitches. If the shape is to be padded leave a small opening and push in the wadding using a stiletto or fine knitting needle. Always use animal wool for the best results; never use cotton wool, which is not soft enough.

Moulds Moulds for hands and faces can be shaped from any good make of modelling clay. Some clays harden on contact with the air and others need to be hardened in an oven for a short while, at a low temperature. The shapes should be kept quite simple; it is best not to attempt to model realistic features on a face. Small holes should be made in the moulds with a needle, so that they can be easily attached to the background in the same way as a bead or button.

Corded filling is made up of rows of buttonhole stitches worked across a thicker thread. The first row is worked along the cord (1). At the end of the row the working thread is taken under and over the edge of the motif and under and over the opposite edge (2). On the next row the needle is placed behind the loop of the stitch above, behind the stretched thread, and formed into a buttonhole stitch (3).

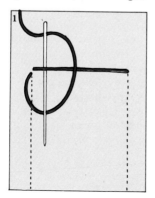

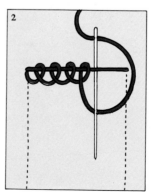

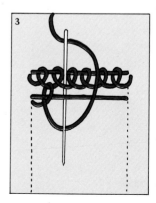

Ceylon Stitch can be worked closely or loosely to give an open effect. Secure a loop of wire to make a free-standing shape and wrap wire with matching thread (**1**). Begin at the left hand top corner of shape and take a foundation thread across the top, through to the back and up again just below the starting point (**2**). On to this work a row of chained loops, then a second row of loops working back into the first row. Repeat backwards and forwards to fill shape (**3**).

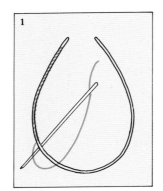 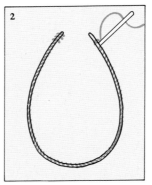 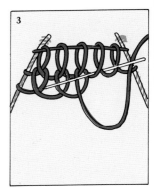

Hollie stitch: work an outline in chain (**1**). Bring thread up through chain loop, carry across to opposite side and pass to the back. Bring up through chain opposite first (**2**). With left thumb on thread pass once round thumb from left to right, buttonhole, passing the needle into row of chain above. Bring down under laid thread and loop encircling thumb (**3**). At end of each line take thread across from left to right. Continue as before.

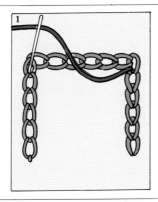 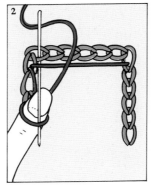 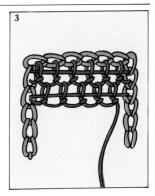

Padded satin stitch gives a raised area of long straight stitches. The direction in which these fall influence the way light is reflected. Cut a felt shape and secure with overcasting stitches; several shapes can be layered for extra padding (**1**). Carefully work straight stitches horizontally across the padded area to completely cover it (**2**). Then work another layer of stitches in the direction required, taking care to keep the outline edges even.

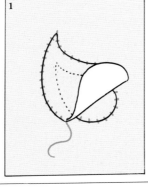 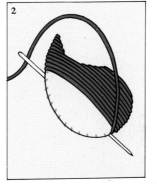 

Rococo stitch: working diagonally from top right to bottom left, insert needle upwards over four horizontal threads and bring out two threads down and one to right. Insert needle to left (**1**). Bring out two threads below. Three more long stitches are worked and crossed in a similar way then the thread is passed downwards behind the adjacent four threads ready to make the next stitch (**2**). When one diagonal line is completed the next is worked beside it until the whole area is covered (**3**).

 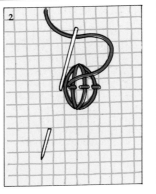 

LEFT: *This panel, called* Esther and Ahasuerus *dated 1686, is a typical example of raised work, with figures in contemporary costume surrounded by a profusion of animals, birds, insects, trees, flowers and fruit. In the centre the king sits under a canopy, holding a sceptre and orb; his hands are shaped from covered wire. The castle in the background has windows of mica; a large lion sits outside, showing a total disregard for scale. Some of the motifs are raised from the surface with padding, and petals and leaves are worked in detached buttonhole stitch. The whole panel is an interesting example of the many different techniques used during the period.*

BELOW: *This modern example shows the use of slips. The trees in the foreground are stitched with French knots on calico; those behind show canvaswork stitches on fine canvas.*

Canvaswork slips Draw out the motif to be worked on either fine soft canvas, or tailor's canvas. Use crewel wool, or silk thread for the embroidery, keeping to simple stitches such as tent, Hungarian, and Gobelin. When the motif is complete, cut it out leaving a small border all round. Tuck this under and stitch the slip in position on the background using small stitches in matching coloured thread.

Slips on calico Textured slips can be worked on calico using closely packed French knots. Use a variety of threads in different thicknesses from matt wools to shiny silks. When the motif is finished cut it out and stitch it down in the same way as the canvas work slip. If extra height is needed the shape can be padded, but the tight cluster of knots should give a sufficient raised effect.

Padding with felt Cut out the shape required, then another slightly smaller and a third smaller again. Begin by sewing the smallest shape in position with tiny stab stitches. Apply the next size over the top and then the third and largest over the two, making three layers of padding. Always bring the needle up through the background fabric and down through the felt; this will prevent the felt tearing. A final layer of fabric or fine kid can be applied or the shape can be covered with detached buttonhole stitch.

Raised shapes over wire By using wire as a framework motifs can be made which stand free of the background,

attached only in one place. Fine craft wire or florist's wire is the most suitable. Cut the required length of wire and wrap it closely and tightly with a soft thread, not wool or a springy silk. Knot the thread around the wire before winding it, and secure it at the other end when the wire is covered. Twist the wire into the desired shape. Tie another thread on, and begin filling in the shape with detached buttonhole stitch, using the wire as if it were fabric. When it is finished, sew the shape in place on the background, tucking the ends through the fabric with the help of a stiletto or a large tapestry needle. Secure with tiny stitches. Clusters of similar shapes may form the petals of flowers or leaves.

Lacy motifs Softer motifs can be worked on muslin which is then cut away. Draw the required shape on to the fabric and oversew a firm thread round it, using the method for 'trailing' in whitework. The stitches must be very close together as when it is finished it should have the effect of fine cord. Using this 'cord' to anchor the thread, work a lacy filling of fine buttonhole bars. Cut out the motif carefully with small pointed scissors keeping close to the edge; turn over and cut the fabric away from the underside. Sew the motif in position on the background. This method gives a delicate effect.

Satin stitch over felt This method gives the same effect as padded satin stitch: a crisp, smooth, slightly raised appearance. Use a thick piece of felt. Cut out the shape and tack it in place on the background fabric. Work the satin stitch over the shape starting from the centre and working outwards. Stranded cotton will give the best result, and the stitches should be worked over and over which means that there will be the same amount of thread on the back as on the front.

ABOVE: *A detail from a seventeenth-century long band sampler, of linen worked in coloured silks and linen threads. Many of the motifs are worked in detached buttonhole stitch.*

LEFT: *A modern example, worked in silk threads on a silk background fabric, which shows the use of a number of techniques. The main stem is raised by couching a bundle of linen threads close together; rows of stem stitch are worked over this foundation to cover the core. The flowers and some of the leaves are worked in detached buttonhole stitch; other leaves are canvaswork slips. The small berries are embroidered in satin stitch over shapes cut from thick bonded interfacing.*

CONTEMPORARY STUMPWORK

Borders make ideal subjects for using simple repeat motifs which can be padded. Shells, flowers, foliage and fruit, and many natural forms, can be raised with layered padding and stitched with shiny threads to great effect.

This embroidered mirror frame worked in silks and stranded cottons on a background of silk fabric shows a border of fruit worked in satin stitch over shapes cut from felt. A mirror tile is used, secured in a thick card.

APPLIQUE

A very apt and telling description of appliqué is given by Lewis F. Day in *Art in Needlework*, published in 1908. 'Appliqué work is thought by some to be an inferior kind of embroidery. That is not so. It is not a lower but another kind of needlework, in which more is made of stuffs than of stitches. In it the craft of the needleworker is not carried to the limit; but, on the other hand, it makes great demands upon design. You cannot begin by just throwing about sprays of natural flowers. It calls peremptorily for treatment — by which test the decorative artist stands or falls. Effective it must be; coarse it may be; vulgar it should not be; trivial it can hardly be. Mere pettiness is outside its scope. It lends itself to dignity of design and nobility of treatment.'

As this description suggests, appliqué work is particularly appropriate in cases where the work has to be seen from a distance (as in church and ceremonial work); its patterns can be readable as far away as its colours can be distinguished.

ABOVE: *A striking example of a typical Hawiian folded quilt. The appliqué motif of light-coloured flowers and leaves is silhouetted by the background of red cotton fabric. In this American quilt the whole area is hand quilted after the appliqué is completed.*

Appliqué has been used, and still is, worldwide. Perhaps the earliest use arose when someone was repairing a tear or a hole by cutting a patch and sewing it to the garment. The words *appliqué* and *onlay* normally refer to applying one textile to another (a textile being a cloth fashioned by using threads). Since ancient times other materials were also employed, eg. felt and bark cloth. Felt and leather appliqué was used by wandering cattle-breeding tribes for religious and ceremonial practices and was held in high esteem even when silk became available. Skins and furs were used by early man for very elaborate applied and inlaid work; similar work is still produced in cold climates in northern countries.

There is an enormous variety of textile appliqué styles in use today. In India, large hangings, carriage cloths and flags are decorated with coloured cotton cloth, often with counterchange designs. The squares which decorate the Indian quilts and ceiling covers are large pieces of cotton cloth, folded and folded again, cut into a pattern, spread out on white calico and then applied. The stitching for ceiling decoration, often hemstitching, may be quite crude, since it is to be viewed from a distance. This method (though with very fine stitching) was also used by German and British colonists in eighteenth- and nineteenth-century America on quilts, where the appliqué technique was often combined with patchwork. In Resht work (from parts of Iran, near the Caspian Sea) a cord or chain stitch is used to cover the joins; it often resembles inlay patchwork. Nomadic hilltribes in Thailand make very delicate appliqué of fine cotton fabric. In western Africa fine leather appliqué and bold designs on cotton cloth are made for religious ceremonies, tribal gatherings, and funerals. Funeral hangings depict events in the life of the deceased.

The Kuna Indians, of the San Blas Islands on the northern coast of Panama, make a type of work called Mola work, which is multi-layered, giving a quilted appearance and allowing a large range of colours to show through in layers in cut-out features. The Eastern Plains and Woodlands Indians of the USA make a form of appliqué work from coloured ribbons (originally imported from France in the eighteenth century).

European appliqué styles include large-scale appliqué, popular during the 1880s, where patches were applied to the ground with chain stitch, and then additional decorative herringbone stitch was worked. Sabrina work used velvet, satin and silk, or washable fabrics, for cut-out flowers and leaves, which were attached with widely spaced buttonhole stitch. Broderie perse is applied work in which figures, trees, flowers and animals and other subjects are cut from cotton cloth and stitched either to a plain ground or to patchwork. Separately worked fine embroidery can be applied to precious textiles.

Techniques

A patch can be applied in various ways. The technique is often determined by the final use of the work; if it is for hard wear, or has to be washed often, it is essential that the method of attaching the patch can stand up to this treatment. On any fabric which frays, the edges must be turned under; when working with felt or leather the edges can be sewn invisibly to the base fabric, or the stitching can be made a feature of the design. The raw edges of a patch can also be finished with close stitching, couching a cord over the join, or by machine satin stitch. Features from printed fabrics can be cut out and applied to a background fabric.

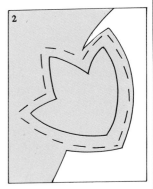
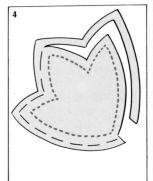
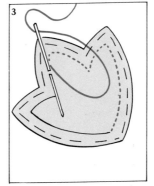

Basic appliqués Pin template to right side of fabric and draw around the outline with a sharpened coloured pencil. Mark a ¼ in (6mm) seam allowance outside the drawn line (**1**). Cut out the motif outside the two lines (**2**). Staystitch just outside the turning line (**3**). Trim fabric to outer marked line (**4**).

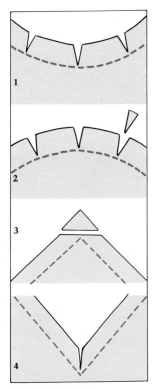

Sewing method 1 Clip into curves and corners. Fold turnings to wrong side and finger press. Tack turnings in place (**1**). Pin patch to main fabric and if needed, secure with vertical tacking stitches to prevent fabrics from wrinkling. Slipstitch in place along folded edge (**2**). Take out tacking threads.

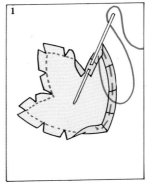

Neatening curves and corners helps to give a really professional finish to your appliqué. On inner curves, clip into seam allowance to staystitching (**1**). On outer curves, cut out notches to prevent bulky pleats forming on underside (**2**). On outside corners, trim point to reduce fabric from mitred corner (**3**). On inner corners, clip into point to staystitching (**4**)

Sewing method 2 Clip into edges of patch and pin in place on main fabric without turning in raw edges. Secure with vertical tacking stitches if needed. Avoid tacking into seam allowance (**1**). Using point of needle to turn raw edge under, slipstitch in place (**2**).

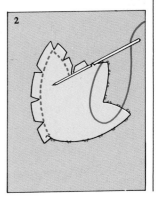

RIGHT: *A detail of a Jain wedding ceiling canopy (Shamiana) from Rajasthan, India. The canopy is made up of nine large squares, eight of which are folded and cut from white cotton fabric which is applied to red cotton. They are joined together with bands of patchwork diamonds and triangles*

BELOW: *This detail of a Meo hilltribe baby carrier from Thialand shows a design of small yellow squares outlined with corners of red cross stitch. Pink squares are superimposed onto the evenweave fabric. Bands of cotton strips have been folded at the corners and machined around the rectangle to form a border. The lining and the panel are held together by pompons formed from loops of pink cotton thread stitched to the work in a tight circle forming a tuft. The loops are then cut.*

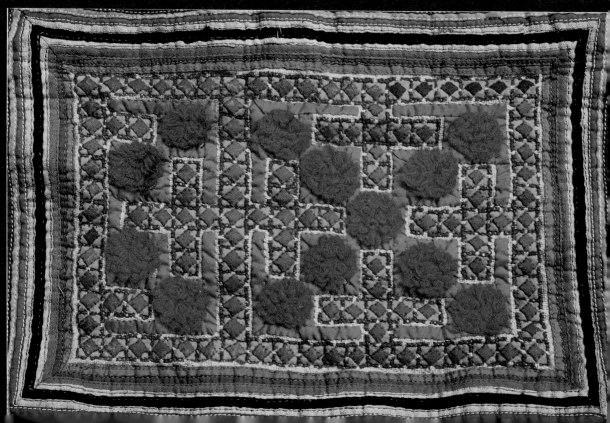

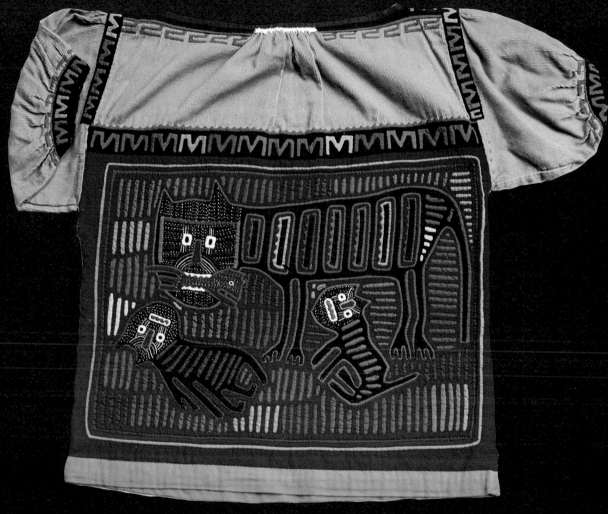

ABOVE: *A Mola blouse built up from a red panel with layers of fabric and coloured patches. The last layer of red is cut and sewn to produce frames, slits and cat shapes which have embroidered faces.*

BELOW: *This Rajasthani bridegroom's bag for carrying sweetmeats has a fine red cotton base, with bands and shapes of white cotton applied with running and blind stitch. It is bordered with bands of yellow and faded blue with zigzag points.*

Inlaid appliqué

Inlay is a form of appliqué in which shapes are cut from the ground fabric, and patches added which fit exactly into the negative shapes created. The two fabrics to be used are placed one on top of the other, and the shape required cut through both layers. This results in counterchange: the shape cut from one layer fits exactly into the other and *vice versa*. The first layer is placed on a background fabric mounted in a frame; the vacant space is filled by the piece from the second layer, and the edges are finally oversewn.

Method This form of inlaid appliqué uses several layers of fabric. Four different layers are used. With ground fabric right side up, apply small diamond-shaped patches in a regular pattern slipstsitching them in place (**2**). Still with ground fabric right side up, tack raw edged patches in place where needed (**3**). Place second layer of fabric right side up on appliqué and pin to hold (**4**). Turn layers over with wrong side of ground fabric facing. Tack around stitched areas leaving required margin between 2/10in (5mm) —

3/10in (8mm)(**5**). Turn appliqué wrong side down. Snip fabric in to corners to tacking stitches (**6**). Trim fabric inside diamonds leaving a small seam allowance (**7**). Turn under edges and slipstitch around (**8**). Leave tacks and apply next layer of fabric as in stage four. Apply remaining layers in this way.

RIGHT: *Shirt yoke worked in Kuna appliqué in diamond patterns on a plain calico ground.*

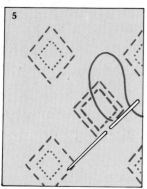

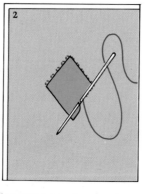
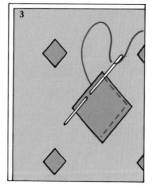
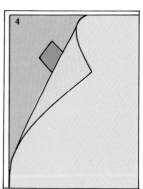
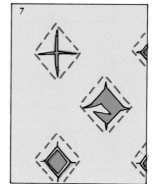
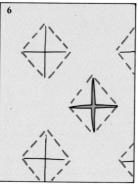
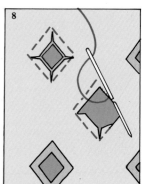

Machine appliqué

As the sewing machine is employed more and more in decorating textiles, its use has naturally spread to appliqué. Interesting effects can be achieved by combining appliqué with free machining, superimposing different fabrics which may be transparent and have coloured threads underneath, for example, and then holding them in place or attaching them to the background with different coloured stitch combinations. The contrast between raw edges and the firm lines of zigzag or satin stitch gives a wide choice in the interpretation of designs. Free machine techniques may be used for applying strips of fabric, braids and ribbons.

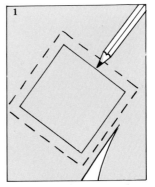

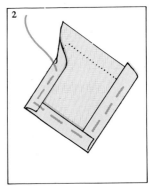

Straight method (right). Pin template to right side of fabric and draw around with a sharpened coloured pencil. Mark a 2/10in (5mm) cutting line outside drawn line and cut out shape beyond this line (**1**). Staystitch just outside the foldline. Trim patch on cutting line. Snip into curves and corners, fold turning to wrong side and tack in place (**2**). Pin and tack patch to main fabric using vertical tacks (**3**). Machine around edge (**4**).

Zigzag method (below): pin template to right side of fabric and draw around outline. Cut out leaving ⅜in-¾in (1cm-2cm) extra fabric all round (**1**). Tack to main fabric with vertical stitches avoiding stitching through extra fabric. Machine stitch on drawn line (**2**). Trim extra fabric back to stitching (**3**). Zigzag stitch over edge (**4**). Neaten ends and remove tacking threads.

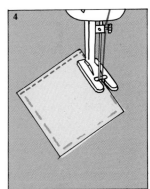

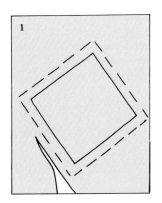

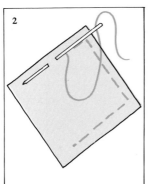

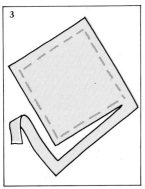

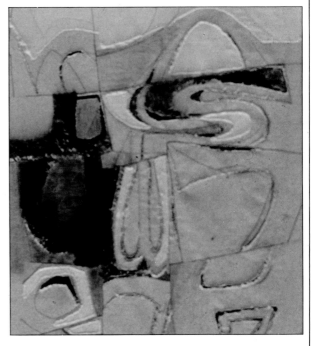

ABOVE: *A modern, machine-appliquéd panel 'Terracotta on white' contrasts the raw edges of plain calico on brown cotton with paint, crayon and hand stitches.*

LEFT: *This Swedish bag, dated 1868 is a simple rectangle made from white leather and decorated on the front with a red and green appliquéd design. The border and applied motifs are cut from felted wool cloth, and these are sewn down with silk threads using back, straight and satin stitches. Some small white buttons are added for further decoration. The back of the bag is left plain and cut higher than the front showing the lining of patterned cotton. A braid shoulder strap is sewn on the top edge at either side.*

LEFT: *This is a fine example of Meo hilltribe appliqué. Regular symmetrical patterns are made by first folding a square of fine cotton in half, folding in half again and then folding diagonally in half. On the final triangle a curved or linear design can be drawn and partly cut through — unfolded, the design will be an eighth-fold repeat. The square is tacked centrally to the ground fabric, the edges turned under with the point of the needle, and stitched to the base. Red patches have been inserted under the corners and in the centre. The tiny running stitches in the remaining spaces are worked from the back of the work. The yellow circles are worked in blanket stitch.*

BELOW *Lisu hilltribe embroidery used extensively on blouse sleeves and yokes. Onto a narrow strip of cotton a second strip is sewn, right sides and edges together, it is turned down, leaving a slight ridge. More strips are added in the same fashion. The triangles are made from rectangles of fabric with the long side turned under and folded in half. The folded corner produces one triangle. The triangles are aligned and covered by the next strip.*

PATCHWORK

This technique, which makes use of small pieces of fabric, has a long history. The earliest known pieces, fragments of silk joined together to make, among other things, a hanging (dated between the sixth and ninth centuries AD), were discovered in the 1920s in a remote part of India. In poor communities throughout history, re-use of the good parts of worn clothing and furnishings has been essential; so simple shapes were devised to make the new article more attractive. Over the years design has become more complex and sophisticated, and different uses found for the work.

Designing for patchwork involves using light, medium and dark tones of the colours chosen, plain and patterned fabrics, so that they show up against each other. Where the patterned fabric is used to create a new pattern, it may not be possible to follow the grain line of the fabric.

Fabrics

Choose a fabric suitable for the final use of the project in hand. A medium-weight cotton is easiest to use, but there is a wide choice of cotton fabrics, from lawn to corduroy and velvet. Add to these wools, silks, and mixtures such as polyester/cotton, and the variety is very wide indeed.

Synthetic fabrics, which do not hold a crease, can be difficult to work. Experiment with different methods of handling them. Washable fabrics should be pre-shrunk before making up, by washing.

Avoid variations of fabric thickness in one piece of work, unless very carefully planned. They can make it difficult to fit the shapes together.

When cutting from a template, it is usual to align one edge with the grain of the fabric. This helps ensure that the finished work will be smooth and unpuckered.

TEMPLATES

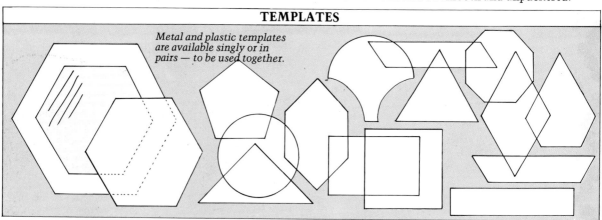

Metal and plastic templates are available singly or in pairs — to be used together.

Handsewn patchwork

Handsewn, or English patchwork, is traditionally made by sewing geometric patches together, often in mixed colours and prints to give a mosaic-like effect. The technique involves sewing the fabric over backing papers, whereby small intricate shapes can be made such as the hexagon, lozenge, diamond and clamshell. Templates of most shapes can be bought from craft suppliers, or you can make your own to suit your design. The finished patches can be stitched together in either a random way or in a variety of patterns. The hexagon, which forms the Grandmother's Flower Garden pattern, is one of the most popular shapes, as is the diamond.

Backing the patches: for hand sewn patchwork, pin paper template to wrong side of patch. Fold edge over and secure with pieces of masking tape. Tack around edges (**1**). Remove tape, press folded edges with toe of iron (**2**) — this makes sewing the patches together much easier.

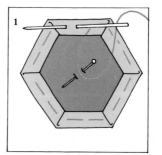

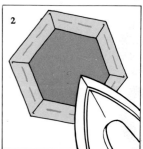

Folding corners: pin paper template to wrong side of fabric, fold over and tack the first side of diamond (**1**). Before folding over second side, fold point of first turning onto second side. Fold and tack second side (**2**). Tack side three as for stage two and then tack side four.

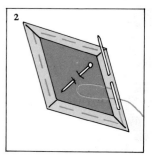

Oversewn patchwork: when all the patches have been prepared join them together with tiny overcasting stitches. Make sure the stitches do not go through the paper backing. Join individual patches placing them right sides together. Secure thread with small back stitch at beginning and end. Join patches into rows first, and then join the rows together.

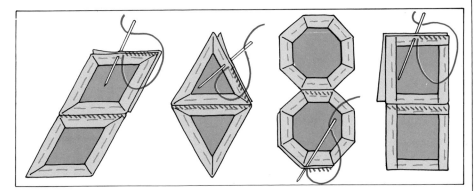

BELOW: *A patchwork quilt of hexagons in the design called 'Grandmother's Flower Garden'.*

RIGHT: *Diamonds in light, medium and dark tones form this all-over 'Tumbling Blocks' design.*

Machine joining patchwork can be done by aligning fabric patches with presser foot. This gives a ¼ in (6mm) seam allowance. The patches should be cut accurately for this. Begin by pinning and machining individual patches together in rows (**1**). Press seams open. Then join rows together (**2**). Join tacked hexagonal patches with zigzag stitch on right side (**3**).

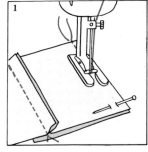

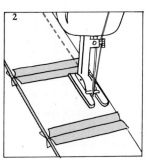

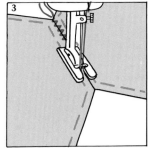

Strip patchwork

Strips of fabric are cut or torn across the width of the chosen fabrics. The strips may be stitched to a backing, or to each other, to produce an area of fabric of the required size. Press each seam before sewing the next.

If working on a backing fabric, use a lightweight cotton or cotton/polyester. Place the first strip right side up across the centre of the backing fabric. Place a second strip, raw edges and right sides together, and stitch taking a ¼ in (6mm) seam. Turn the second strip over, and press.

Repeat these two stages until that side is complete, then repeat for the other half.

This type of patchwork can be made up by the block method. When using this method, work on all the blocks in sequence, so that any new fabric that needs to be introduced appears in every block in some way.

The strips can be applied vertically, horizontally, or diagonally. Take great care while stitching strips on the diagonal, as they may easily pucker. A layer of wadding can be placed on the backing fabric, and the strips stitched in place through both fabrics.

A variety of fabrics can be used, contrasting matt with shiny, textured with smooth. The width of the strips can also be varied.

RIGHT: *Strips of plain and patterned cotton, silks and satins are pieced together to make this attractive quilted hanging. The strips, which vary greatly in length, are combined with lengths of pieced fabric, resembling lines of small squares or triangles. Lengths of covered piping cord are inserted into some of the seams to enrich the surface.*

ABOVE: *This detail of a twentieth century Turkoman tent-hanging from Afghanistan shows a patchwork of richly coloured and textured fabrics. Some of the pieces are of ikat-dyed silk, where the pattern is made by dyeing the warp threads before the fabric is woven. Other fabrics used include felt, velvet and strips of patterned braid.*

RIGHT: *This American quilt is a typical example of crazy patchwork. A rich variety of fabrics has been used, further embellished by the use of surface stitches to embroider small motifs, and the ornamentation of the seams of the pieced fabric by a variety of stitches, including variations of feather, herringbone, and buttonhole. The quilt is made up of a series of square blocks of crazy patchwork, joined together and surrounded by a striking decorative border.*

Crazy patchwork

This method, much favoured by the Victorians, involves the use of irregular fabric shapes stitched to a backing. Mark the required shape on the backing fabric (calico or sheeting). Turn in the frayed edges of the fabric scraps. Starting in one corner, lay the shapes down, overlapping the edges or turning under a narrow hem. Secure with small running stitches. Embroider the joins if required.

Alternatively, crazy patchwork can be made in the following way. Arrange a colourful selection of mixed plain and patterned unneatened patches on ground fabric and tack in place with small stitches (1). Complete tacking patches in position and cover edges with a decorative embroidery stitch. Use couching, feather or herringbone stitch for example (2).

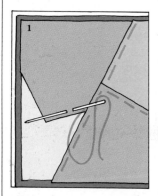

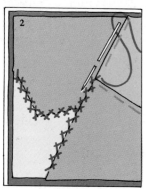

ABOVE: *The Victorian love of elaborate decoration can be seen in this example of crazy patchwork, made with different coloured scraps of silk and satin. The surface is covered with couched metallic cord, sequins and beads.*

Seminole patchwork
This method evolved among the Seminole Indians during the late nineteenth-century. Its development was influenced by the introduction of the sewing machine.

When working this method, it is easiest to choose a fabric that does not fray and will press flat. Stitch together at least three fabric strips of varying widths. Cut the pieced strip, at right angles or 45°, into identical sections, and rejoin, altering the arrangement of the original fabrics by off-setting, reversing, and so on.

BELOW: *Seminole patchwork is most effective when used in small quantities, as can be seen in its use on this cream-coloured calico cushion with other cotton fabrics in medium and dark tones. The final pieced fabric is cut into radiating diagonal shapes, which are moved to create yet more shapes.*

Shell patchwork

Shell patchwork, also known as Clam shell or Fish scale patchwork, derives its name from the shape of the templates. Metal templates are available in pairs: the smaller one is used for cutting the paper backing and the larger one for cutting the fabric which includes the seam allowance. To make your own template, see the diagrams below. Choose soft, firmly woven fabrics and use a matching thread for joining the patches. The simple repeating pattern can be varied by experimenting with tones and colours. You may also wish to experiment by joining patches together on a background fabric using machine zigzag stitch.

How to make shell patches; first make a paper template by drawing a circle on graph paper using a pair of compasses. Mark centre of circle both ways. Then draw two arcs at each side of bottom section just inside the centre lines. Cut out the shell template, as shown in a darker colour, in the diagram opposite.

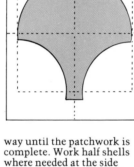

How to join shell patches: assemble the completed patches in your planned pattern. Lay the top row right side up on a soft surface — an ironing board or clean floor space is ideal — and pin in place. Make sure the top edges are in a straight line and sides touching (**1**). Then position the second row of patches on top overlapping the bottom half of the shells, and tack in place. Neatly slipstitch around the curved edges joining the two rows together (**2**). Continue in this way until the patchwork is complete. Work half shells where needed at the side edges. On the last row, trim the bottom half of the shells, turn under seam allowance and tack across ready for finishing (**3**). Take out tacking stitches.

Suffolk puffs

Suffolk Puffs are gathered circular patches which are handsewn together with the edges touching and leaving small spaces in between. The most effective fabrics to use are fine ones such as silk, soft cotton voile or organdie. The gathered side of the circle is the right side and the central hole creates a decorative, textural effect. This simple technique can be varied in several ways: combine puffs of different sizes in one project or place a decorative filling in transparent puffs. The gathering thread need not be pulled tight, thus showing the inside of the patch, which could be padded or filled with a contrasting colour, or stitched varying the length of the connecting stitches.

Patch making: this method of using a paper template means that the same one can be used to make several shell patches. Cut out fabric patches allowing an extra ¼ in (6mm) seam allowance all round. Pin paper backing to right side of fabric. Snip into curved edge, fold to wrong side using template edge as a guide for the foldline. Tack through fabric only and remove the paper backing.

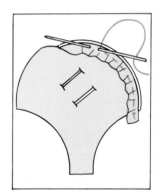

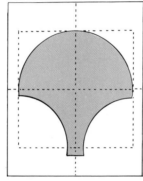

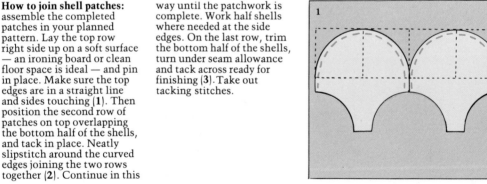

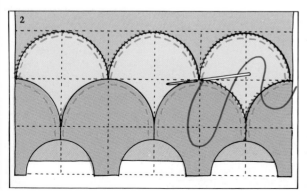

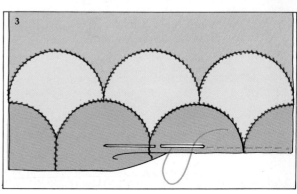

Suffolk puffs make an open, lacy type of patchwork. Begin by cutting circles of fabric about twice the diameter of the finished patch. Fold over a ¼ in (6mm) turning to wrong side, and using a strong thread secured firmly, run even gathering stitches around the edge (**1**). Pull up the gathering thread tightly. Flatten the shape so that the gathered edge is in the middle and fasten off thread (**2**).

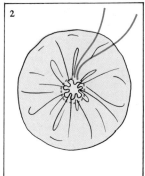

LEFT: *This charming example of Suffolk puffs shows a number of variations on the basic technique. A soft, semi-transparent fabric is used; the long ends of the silk gathering threads add delicacy to the piece. The puffs are stitched closely together in rows, which are then joined again with longer thread covered with small shiny beads.*

Cathedral window patchwork which is also known as Mayflower Patchwork, is traditionally made using calico as the main fabric. The centre patches can be cut from oddments of fabric and these can be of any texture or pattern. Remember when choosing your colour scheme, to select contrasting colours for the patches to give a bright, stained-glass window effect. The main squares use a considerable amount of fabric, so careful planning is needed. The traditional cotton fabric will take a crease easily so the initial turnings could be just pressed, but any fabric that is springy or slippery will need tacking. It is useful to back the centre squares of fabric with an iron-on bonded facing. When folding the edges over the patches stitch with a matching thread to secure them. By making sure that the thread passes through all the layers the work is securely held and a pleasing quilted effect is achieved.

RIGHT: *Cream-coloured satin is used as the main fabric for this cushion in cathedral window patchwork, with toning velvet for the centres.*

Making the patches: begin by cutting sufficient squares of plain-coloured fabric about twice the size of the finished square — 6½ in (16cm) is a practical size. Make ¼ in (6mm) turnings all round and hem in place (**1**). Fold the four corners to the middle and press flat. Pin to secure (**2**). Repeat, folding the corners of the smaller square to the middle and press flat (**3**). Stitch corners at middle. Complete all the squares and stitch together along the sides (**4**). Cut out small squares of contrast fabric ¼ in (6mm) smaller than the diamond formed between the two squares. Pin the fabric on top of the seam between joined squares. Turn the folded edges of the squares over the fabric patch and hemstitch through all layers of fabric (**5**).

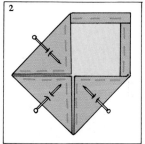

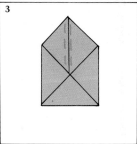

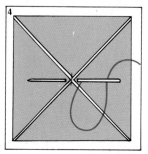

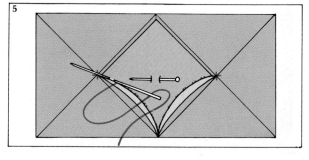

Folded star patchwork is made by attaching folded triangles of fabric in pattern. Begin by cutting sufficient squares of fabric about 2in (5cm) inside. To make triangles, fold square in half (**1**). Fold top corners to centre of base (**2**). Press triangle flat (**3**). Make other triangles. Mark foundation fabric through straight and diagonal centres. Pin first triangle in place and sew point to backing with a tiny stitch (**4**). Add three more triangles and stitch in middle. Attach with running stitch 2/10in (5mm) inside edge (**5**). Now add eight contrast coloured triangles about ⅜in (1 cm) from middle, overlapping corners (**6**), sew as before. Add eight triangles next, sixteen on next two rows, and so on, to finish.

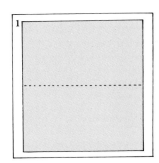
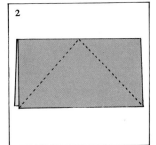
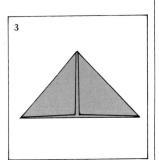
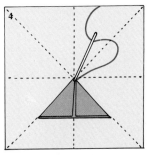
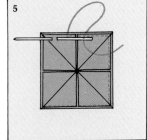
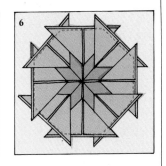

LEFT: *This attractive cushion made of folded star patchwork explores the relationship of patterned dark and light cotton fabrics. The folded squares are built up to give a strong central design reminiscent of a kaleidoscope.*

Logcabin patchwork

Log cabin patchwork is a classic American pattern. It is an economic method as quite small oddments of fabric can be used. The design depends a great deal on the placing of the light and dark fabric strips arranged in blocks. Various names have been given to these patterns, for example: Barn Raising, and Straight Furrow. The central square, traditionally of red fabric, represents the chimney of the the log cabin, and the surrounding strips are rows of logs.

Random patchwork

This method requires a backing fabric (lightweight calico and polyester-cotton are both suitable) and a selection of irregular-shaped fabric pieces in the chosen colour scheme. Cut the backing fabric to the shape of the project with ample turnings.

RIGHT: *Some of the random patches are overlaid with coloured gauze which softens the printed fabric in contrast to the log cabin border.*

ABOVE: *A nineteenth-century quilt in the 'Straight Furrow' pattern which is a variation of the basic log cabin design. The blocks are very large in this particular quilt and the cotton fabric is in strong colours of red, brown and yellow.*

RIGHT: *The cotton fabrics for this contemporary cushion are specially dyed and space-dyed in soft, blending tones.*

Making the patches involves sewing strips of fabric in light and dark sequence around a central square to form a larger square (**1**). Cut backing fabric to size and mark diagonally both ways. Using small running stitches, apply central square (**2**). Cut strips ¼ in (6mm) longer at each end. Stitch strip right side down (**3**). Fold back, apply next strip (**4**), repeat sequence (**5**), and complete patch (**6**).

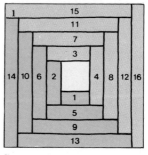

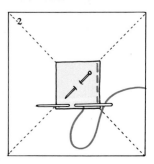

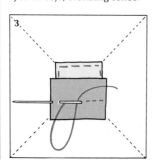

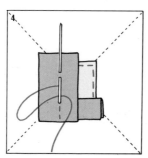

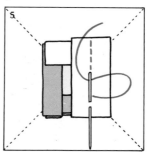

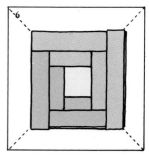

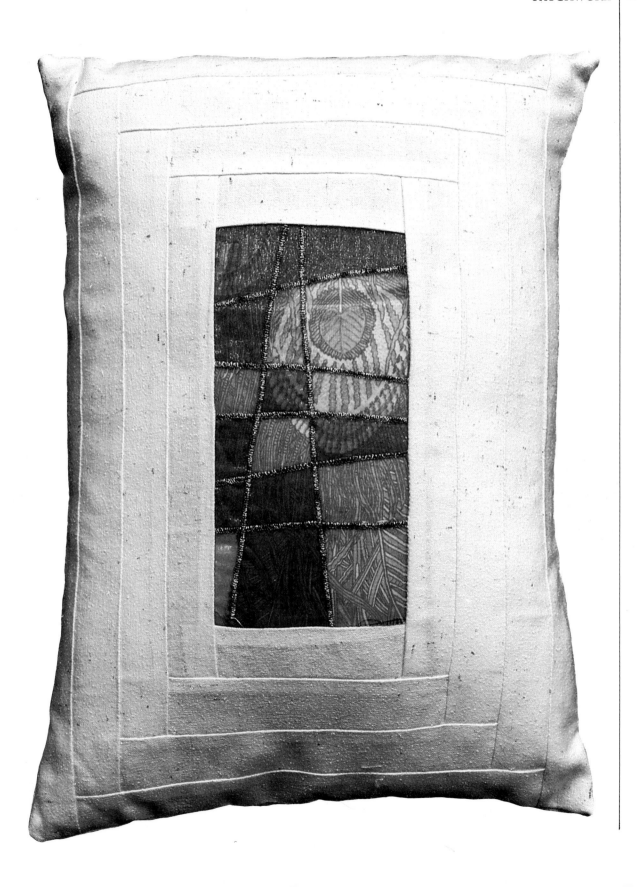

Block Patchwork

Compared with the intricate shaping of hand-sewn patchwork, block patchwork is often bolder in shape and more closely associated with traditional American pieced-block patterns. Here, groups of geometric shapes are sewn into blocks which are then stitched together to make a large patchwork — either by hand or machine, usually without backing papers. The early American settlers gave names to their patterns such as Clay's Choice, Variable Star and Pin Wheel, many of which are still being made today.

Finishing

All patchwork should be well finished. It is usually lined and often quilted. The treatment of the edges is an important part of finishing. Plain coloured borders in varying depths with either mitred or square corners can be added. Piped edges can be very effective; choose one of the fabrics used in the patchwork itself to provide continuity of colour. Folded star patches can make an effective edge for garments and wall hangings. Tabs, fringes and tassels can be used to decorate the edges of hangings, quilts and cushions.

Quilts are usually finished with a bound edge. Make a fabric sleeve on the wrong side of a quilt, for display. It is traditional to date and sign a quilt. For an unquilted wall hanging, back with pelmet-weight bonded interfacing.

Finishing patchwork involves pressing the whole area on a padded surface. A well-padded work table is ideal for large items. Place patchwork right side down and pin to surface through patches along each side (**1**). Press under a damp cloth with moderate heat (**2**). Take out tacking threads and paper patches — to be used again if not damaged (**3**).

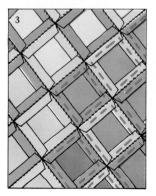

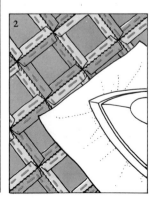

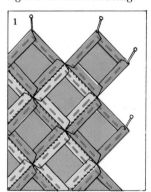

PIECED BLOCK

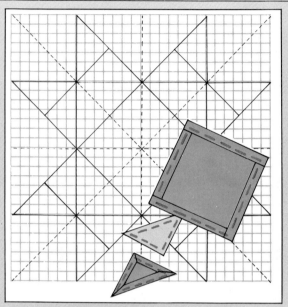

To construct this traditional block draw the pattern to the correct size on graph paper. Cut out the different templates to be used and glue them to thin card. Place the templates on the wrong side of the fabric, draw round and cut out with ⅜in (6mm) seam allowance. The smaller pieces of the block are sewn together first, right sides together using small running or machine stitches on the sewing line. Join all the units together to complete the block.

This is a good example of an American pieced block called Missouri Star.

ABOVE: *Cream, orange and pink cotton fabrics are used for this Feathered Star patterned quilt worked towards the end of the last century. Some of the triangular pieces are minute, and the quilt has been beautifully and very finely sewn throughout.*

WHITEWORK

Fine whitework has flourished through the centuries, all over the world; from China and India to Italy, Scandinavia, Germany and Great Britain. Sometimes it has had a place in the ascendancy of fashion, but it has also been constantly used for decorating household linen and the fair linen used in the church.

There are basically two types of whitework: coarse and fine. Coarse work, on opaque fabric, involves surface embroidery, in addition to drawing out threads, cutting holes, or drawing threads together to make lacy patterns. Cutwork, Hardanger, Hedebo, Mountmellick and reticella are all forms of coarse work.

Fine work is sewn on sheer fabrics, such as organdie, lawn, muslin, glass cambric, and net. Ayrshire, Carrickmacross, *chikan* work (from India), Dresden (from Germany) and shadow appliqué work are examples of fine work.

'Fine whitework is perhaps the most artistic pursuit in the world, and you must realise this and be glad it is so.' These words were written by Lady Evelyn Murray (1868-1940), who sewed the finest whitework in Britain, which may be seen at Blair Castle, Perthshire. It is worked on glass cambric; one sampler shows no less than eleven exquisite patterns.

LEFT: *This typical example of Hardanger work shows the bold pattern created by the kloster blocks.*

BELOW: *The cut shapes of this Hedebo stye of embroidery are decorated with needle-made fillings. Motifs in* padded satin stitch are worked on the surface of the fine linen.

BOTTOM: *This fine example of needle-made filling shows the typical seventeenth century geometric design of early reticella.*

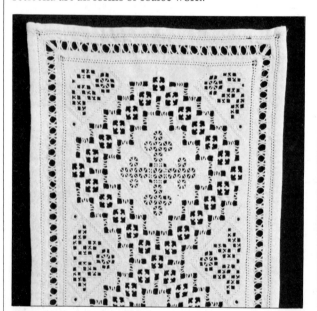

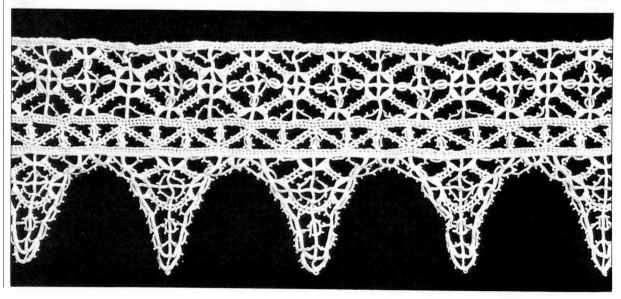

Ayrshire Whitework

Ayrshire Whitework, also called 'The Flowering', was one of the few forms of whitework to develop on a commercial scale, flourishing from the 1820s to the 1860s.

Whitework was introduced to Ayrshire by Mrs Jamieson of Ayr, a sewn muslin agent, who had seen a whitework christening robe brought from France by Lady Mary Montgomerie in 1814, and thought there might be a market for such fine work produced in Scotland. She built up a cottage industry on a basis of the workers' previous knowledge of tamboured muslin work, which preceded whitework as a commercial venture in the west of Scotland.

Whitework became a favourite and profitable local industry, although its promoters and the art-trained designers were not local, coming mainly from Glasgow and Paisley. The work was mainly used for fashionable accessories: cuffs, collars, shirt frills, christening robes, and bonnets were typical products.

Very fine cotton thread was used, and locally-woven cotton lawn (muslin). The crowns of babies' bonnets were sewn on sheer linen cambric. The patterns were scrolled, floral, and so intricate that the best pieces had the appearance of lace. The stitches used were stem, padded satin, trailing, close buttonhole, and eyelets; cut parts of the design were filled with fine needlepoint lace fillings. This is the hallmark of Ayrshire work.

The designs were professionally drawn and at first printed on the muslin with wood blocks and rollers rubbed with a blue bag. Then this muslin was delivered to the outworkers. Later a lithographic press was used.

Old records show that 'The Flowering' could be a profitable as well as an enjoyable occupation. The earnings of the embroiderers, on piece-work rates, compared favourably to those of carpenters, builders and farm workers. The most intricate work was given to the best needlewomen, and the garment was sent to be made up in Paisley or Glasgow. The 'Floo'erers', who were said to love their work, also embroidered christening robes and bonnets for their own and relatives' children, copying the professional designs and making up the garments themselves.

The bodice of a christening robe was designed with a V-shaped panel from shoulders to waist, coming to a point where it joined the skirt. (For a girl, the point was tucked into the garment; for a boy, it remained outside.) The design on the skirt was in the form of an inverted V, with the weight of the design coming down to the hem.

In all commercial work the purchaser paid for the quality. Agents had detailed samplers, and purchasers specified the quality and amount of work and of needlepoint fillings when ordering. It is mistaken to

ABOVE: *A nineteenth-century English bonnet. The crown is of Valenciennes lace with points of needlepoint fillings.*
The sidebands are alternating bands of Ayrshire embroidery and Valenciennes lace.

attribute the best work to any particular period; once the industry was established, money bought the best quality.

At its height, trade was so extensive, that sewing was sent out of Ayrshire, to other parts of Scotland and even to Northern Ireland. The decline of the industry coincided with the interruption of the cotton trade caused by the US Civil War, and the introduction of Swiss machine embroidery, which both made large-scale hand industries less commercially viable.

Eyelet stitch is best worked by counting the threads of the ground fabric. Bring needle out, make a back stitch two threads to right and bring out at starting point (**1**). Insert needle three threads down and one across bringing out three threads across and one up. Pull thread firmly (**2**). Take needle to starting point and bring out in central hole (**3**). Complete the circle working in this way. Work in rows across.

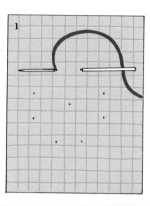

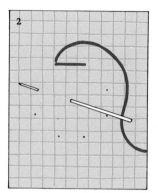

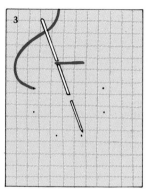

ABOVE: *A white cotton bag in Mountmellick work showing raised blackberries which are* *very characteristic of this type of work.*

Mountmellick

Mountmellick work originated in Ireland as a cottage industry. It differs from other types of whitework in as much as there are no drawn or open spaces. The majority of the stitches lie on the surface with very little showing on the wrong side; the bold surface stitchery is sewn with coarse cotton thread on linen or sateen. Traditionally it has either a knitted fringe or a heavy buttonhole edge. It has been used mostly for household or church linen. The designs are based on flowers and leaves; a variety of stitches is used, including Gordian knot, thorn, bullion, fern, feather and trellis, and the work has a raised effect.

Three-sided stitch is made up of pairs of back stitches pulled firmly. Bring needle out and make two back stitches to right over four threads (**1**). With needle at starting point, make two back stitches diagonally downwards to right over the same number of threads (**2**). Bring needle out four threads to left (**3**). Make two back stitches (**4**). Then work back stitches diagonally up to right and continue in this way to row end (**5**).

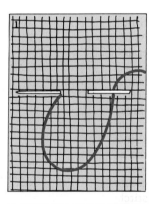

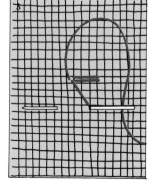

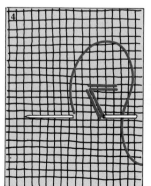

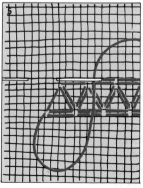

Feather stitch, including double feather, are popular outline stitches. Bring needle out and holding thread to left, make a diagonal stitch a little below centre. Bring out with thread under needle (**1**). Make a similar stitch at the opposite side (**2**) and continue in this way to row end. For double feather stitch, work three loops first and then two loops in alternate directions (**3**).

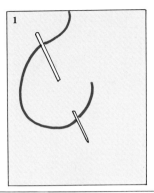
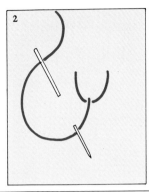
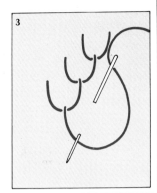

Thorn stitch gives the effect of a thorned branch. Bring needle out at the bottom of the 'branch', insert it at the top and bring out again diagonally to right. Make a diagonal stitch just above the long thread and bring needle out diagonally above (**1**). Make a similar stitch over the long thread and bring out to right (**2**). Repeat from stage one working crossed stitches over the long thread (**3**) to complete the branch.

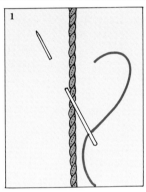
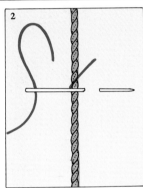
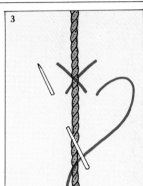

Shadow Work

As its name implies, shadow work is a delicate form of embroidery. Traditionally worked in white on white, it uses semi-transparent fabrics through which stitches or fabric shapes can be seen to form a shadow effect, giving variety of tone. Modern work often incorporates coloured threads and fabrics.

Little seems to be known of the development of shadow work. It has been suggested that it originated in the East and there are similarities to the Indian chikan work, now centred in Lucknow, which sometimes combines shadow work with open work and surface stitchery. In older work double back stitch makes the shadowed areas of the design; the 'Indian' shadow stitch, which is worked slightly differently, may have been used at a later date by some embroiderers for speed or economy.

A form of shadow work appeared in the eighteenth century, worked on muslin and combined with surface embroidery. In this instance the shadow effect was achieved by applying fabric shapes either behind or to the front of the muslin. The Victoria and Albert Museum, in London, possesses some aprons incorporating this technique, which also reflect the oriental influence on design at this period. These muslin aprons formed part of the fashionable woman's dress and were not intended for practical use. Some Dresden work used double back stitch to give opaque shapes contrasting with other stitchery.

In the first half of the twentieth century, some very dainty work was produced, but it was often poor in design and lacking in imagination. Shadow work enjoyed a vogue during the 1920s and 1930s and was much used for mats, tablecloths, dressing table sets, collars, blouses, handkerchiefs and delicate lingerie. For these purposes fine cotton lawn, silk or crêpe de chine were used as well as organdie; babies' gowns, pillowslips and cot covers were worked on robing muslin. The background fabric was usually white, and it was sometimes worked in white, but often brightly coloured threads were used, which on the right side of the work gave the appearance of pastel tints outlined in a brighter colour. For the designs sprays of leaves and flowers were much in favour. Sometimes coloured shapes — leaves, petals or geometric shapes — were applied at the back of the work with pin stitching (also called lace stitch or three-sided stitch) which gave an openwork decorative edge to the shape.

Since the Second World War embroiderers have used shadow work methods more freely, with some interesting results. Man-made fibres have brought the introduction of new fabrics. Painting, spraying and dyeing can be combined with stitchery and stitches themselves are sometimes reversed, so that in parts of the work the threads are seen on the right side of the fabric and in others they are seen through it. Parts of a design may also be cut away to reveal what lies behind. Colours are bolder for both fabric and threads and black can be particularly effective.

ABOVE: *A detail from a twentieth-century whitework organdie runner illustrating the history of costume. There is a great variety of stitches, and in places double or treble pieces of organdie are applied to give a contrast of tone.*

RIGHT: *A corner of an eighteenth-century neckerchief in fine white muslin. The elaborate floral design is outlined in shadow work and there is a great variety of pulled and counted thread fillings. The edge is scalloped and worked in close buttonhole stitch.*

EXPERIMENTING WITH SHADOW WORK

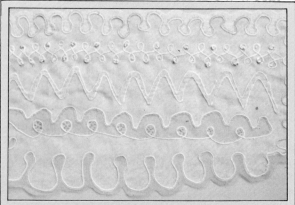

To design a small panel use a sketch or photograph of flowers or foliage. Prepare a background by damping a transparent fabric, and lightly sketch in an impression of the chosen picture in inks or watercolours. The colour will run on the damp surface, and give some unexpected effects. Freely cut shapes and tear strips in a variety of fabrics, some sheer, some opaque. Experiment with these pictures by overlapping and placing them both behind and in front of the background fabric. When you are satisfied with the arrangement of the pieces, anchor them with small invisible stitches. Add some free stitching here and there to suggest the texture of foliage, but do not try to be over-naturalistic.

This example uses layers of coloured organdie which have been cut away in places to reveal a different colour. It is machined in whip stitch with a shaded thread and French knots have been added in silk.

Needlepoint Lace Fillings

The word 'lace', derived from the Latin *laqueus*, meaning loop or noose, originally referred to the cords or braids which were used for lacing garments during the fifteenth century. Since the sixteenth century, 'lace' has also applied to an ornamental openwork fabric.

Needlepoint lace, which is closely related to embroidery, was developed in the sixteenth century from its early origins in simple cut and drawn thread work. Italy, particularly Venice, became its greatest centre, producing and exporting throughout Europe lace of supreme design and workmanship.

Reticella (Latin, *rete*, meaning net) the earliest needlepoint lace, was carried to its extreme, leaving only a skeleton upon which to build a pattern. This fragile foundation was supported by tacking through a sheet of parchment upon which the design was marked, and two layers of linen. Additional bars were made by couching threads through the layers. Using the original withdrawn threads, the pattern was built upon this scaffolding by whipping, needleweaving and buttonhole stitches. When completed, the lace was released from its backing by snipping the tacking with a sharp knife between the layers, thus protecting the lace. Owing to the limitations of working within a grid, reticella designs were always geometric.

From reticella developed the technique known as *punto in aria* (stitch in air) which led to all the beautiful needlepoint laces of the next three centuries. Narrow borders were added to the reticella panels by extending and working upon couched threads beyond the linen foundation. Workers soon dispensed with the foundation altogether, and the lace was built entirely 'in air' upon couched threads. Freed from geometric restrictions, designs could follow flowing lines; scallops and floral motifs were introduced, culminating into the exquisitely beautiful Venetian rose point of the baroque period in the latter half of the seventeenth century.

ABOVE: *A fine example of a seventeenth-century linen cuff 4in (10cm) in depth with a wide lace edging. The design is of squares filled with formal flowers in the reticella style. The points of the cuff are worked in the technique known as* punto in aria.

Techniques

Designs for needlepoint lace should be rounded and flowing, and based on textured shapes and open spaces.

Draw the design, in Indian ink on to architect's linen or thick paper. Cover with coloured adhesive library film. Tack the drawing onto two layers of coarse linen or cotton fabric. This forms the foundation.

Take two or three lengths of thread and lay them over the design. Using a sharp needle threaded with a fine sewing cotton, couch down the laid threads, taking the stitches through all three foundation layers. Keep the couching stitches at right angles to the laid threads. Needlepoint fillings are chiefly based on detached buttonhole stitch. Linear patterns of needleweaving and whipped bars may be incorporated.

Commence filling at the top edge of a shape. Each line of stitching is connected to the outline by a tiny whipping stitch. To keep fillings taut, stretch the lace slightly before finally attaching to the base of the shape.

After completing all the fillings, cover outline edge with close buttonhole stitches. To give the outline extra padding, layers of thread may be laid before covering with the final buttonholing. This is known as *cordonner*.

Finally detach the lace from its foundation by snipping the couching threads between the layers, and carefully removing the loose ends.

RIGHT: *Two elaborately worked reticella panels can be seen in this detail from an early seventeenth-century cutwork sampler. Worked on hand-spun and woven linen, the sampler shows in its design of figures and circular patterns an advanced form of the reticella technique. The skeleton grid of cut and drawn threads upon which the pattern is formed can be clearly seen in the top panel. The addition of loops and picots worked around the* bars give a lacy effect to the bottom panel, which is worked on an even larger grid. The needle-made filling stitches are worked in solid areas which give the appearance of fabric.

Early samplers were worked in a series of strips which often run from the simplest to the most complicated form of the technique.

MATERIALS

Choose firm supple thread both for the filling stitches and the outline. Crochet cotton, no. 70 or finer according to the fineness or coarseness of the design, fine linen lace threads or DMC *fil à dentelles* are all suitable.

Apart from the preliminary couching stitches, the lace is worked on the surface only, the needle never penetrating the foundation. To eliminate the danger of stitch-splitting, use a fine tapestry or ball point needle when working the fillings and edges.

A small pair of sharp pointed scissors is necessary.

Method: to work needle — point motifs, draw the outline on smooth paper. Cut a piece of calico twice size of design, fold in half and tack together with design on top (**1**). Couch a thick thread around outline with sewing cotton stitching 1/10in (2mm) apart (**2**). Using a ballpoint needle and fine thread, work rows of buttonhole loops to fill area (**3**). See variations below.

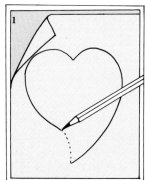
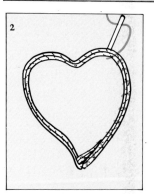
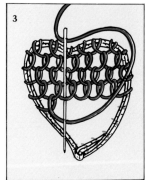

Variation on buttonhole filling: first fold cord in half and beginning with the looped end, couch as above. Finish by threading end through loop. Fold back, trim and stitch to cord. Secure thread to cord and work buttonhole loops over cord only (**1**). Continue to work pairs of loops to end (**2**). Slip needle through cord and work row back making pairs of loops through single loop of previous row (**3**).

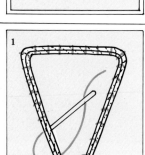
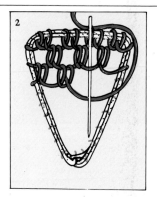

Plain buttonhole bar: these bars are used extensively in needle-made lace. Secure thread by overcasting tape at left side. Take thread to opposite side, stitching through tape. Repeat twice (**1**). Working from right to left, make buttonhole stitches over bar working them close together (**2**). Secure last stitch into edge of tape (**3**).

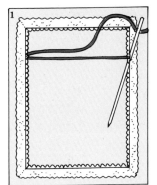
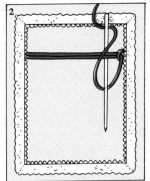
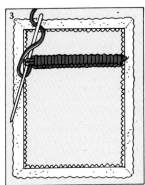

Stepped buttonhole bar gives a very lacy effect. Begin by fastening thread along top edge. Secure a single diagonal stitch to right edge. Make about eight buttonhole stitches over the thread (**1**). Secure thread to opposite side a little lower down (**2**). Work eight buttonhole stitches over thread and continue working from side to side in this way to end (**3**).

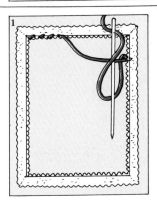
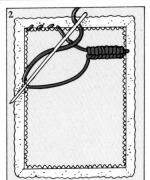
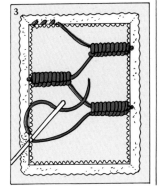

EXPERIMENTING WITH WHITEWORK

In addition to traditional geometric borders, natural forms can be simplified to provide excellent shapes for needlepoint fillings.

The fillings used in this tree-shape design are, working anticlockwise from the top, treble Brussels, pea, hollie point and corded filling stitch.

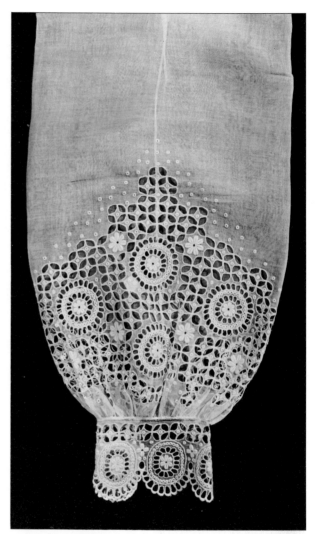

ABOVE: *An English nineteenth-century false sleeve of fine white cotton. A characteristic repeat design* of broderie anglaise lace fillings and scalloped edges.

Making cut shapes: to make eyelets, first work running stitches around traced line — fine coton à broder is an ideal thread to use (1). Snip across the middle both ways. Turn fabric to wrong side and overcast around edges (2). Using sharp embroidery scissors, trim fabric away close to stitching (3) but not so close as to cut through stitching.

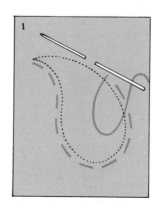

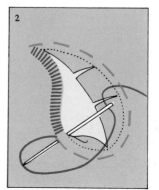

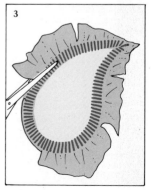

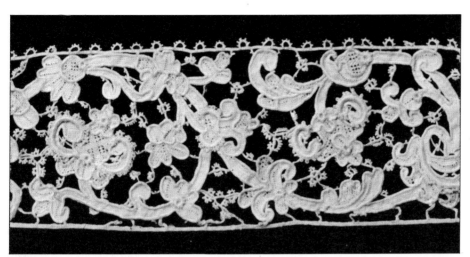

LEFT: *The design of this border typifies the richness of the Baroque period. The cordonnet is covered with buttonholing, and in places is edged with tiny buttonholed picots. The fillings are worked in variations of detached buttonhole stitch.*

BELOW: *A piece of nineteenth-century cutwork is used to make a twentieth-century child's dress. Circular motifs of cut drop shapes decorate the skirt interspersed with eyelets. A border of padded satin stitch leaf sprays are worked above the scalloped edge. Small flower motifs decorate the sleeves and bodice.*

METAL THREAD

One of the earliest mentions of the use of gold for in-darning and weaving is in a description of an ephod (a surplice worn by a Jewish priest) made for Aaron (Exodus XXXIX 2-3). Embroidered and in-woven golden textiles are mentioned in both the Iliad and the Odyssey, and throughout the centuries writers have thought it worth mentioning the use of gold for robes and cloths. The majority of the threads used were silver-gilt or pure silver, pure gold being rarely used. The Durham stole and maniple (AD 909-916) is pure gold thread, but all the *opus anglicanum* ('the English work' as it became known throughout Europe) was in silver-gilt. From the mid-thirteenth century to the middle of the fourteenth century, this mainly professional, largely ecclesiastical work reached an exceptionally high standard of design and technique, excelling in underside and surface couching. During the fourteenth century, following the

Plague and the death of so many embroiderers, there was a noticeable decline in skill. The emphasis changed to secular and domestic embroidery, as the vigorous designs of the Tudor and Elizabethan period developed. Braid and plaited stitches, buttonhole fillings and interlaced knotted stitches were worked in a fine passing thread. Metal threads found their way into canvaswork and blackwork; plate, cut purl and spangles were used to enrich garments. Metal thread work designs were influenced by imports from India and China during the seventeenth and eighteenth centuries respectively — some embroideries showing large-scale figurative compositions. The nineteenth century saw a deterioration in both design and technique with braids, fringes, tassels and cords doing much of the embellishing. Laid work is to be found on Victorian ecclesiastical robes and cloths, still in use today.

ABOVE: *The design on this contemporary red silk chasuble is embroidered in a combination of hand and machine techniques. However, the jap gold and padded kid in the central motif are applied by hand.*

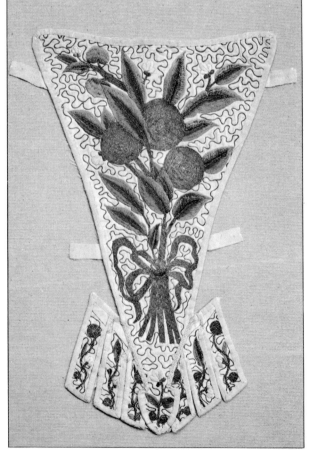

ABOVE: *A seventeenth century stomacher — used to fill in the bodices of dresses. The motif combines silk and metal thread couched in spirals for the flowers, while meandering lines form a background pattern.*

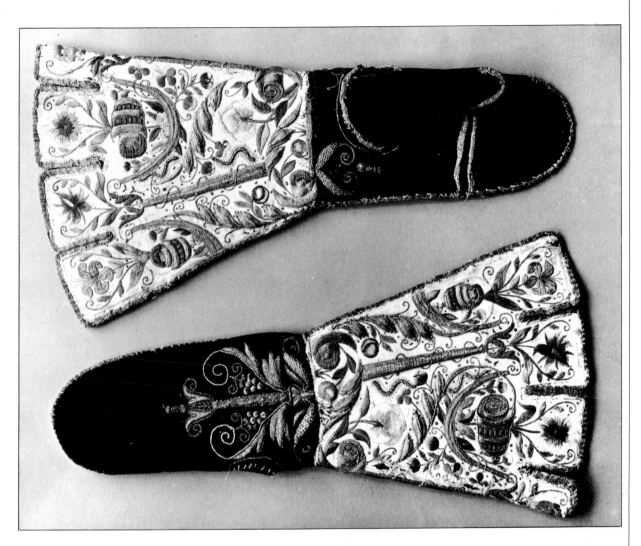

The beauty in a piece of metal thread work lies not only in the perfection of the technique but in the design. As in other types of embroidery, the area is broken up into varied shapes that combine to make a pleasing and harmonious whole. It is a temptation in any form of embroidery to use too many different threads, fillings and textures, which may make an excellent sampler for reference but which do not build up into a unified piece of work. The temptation is even stronger in metal thread embroidery as it so often depends on one colour with variation of tone. The beauty of the technique lies in the play of light over the varied undulating surfaces of the threads and cords, giving highlights and depths of tone in pleasing shapes. The lay of the threads should follow the form of the design, giving it life and movement. Areas of richness are often set off to advantage by being laid against simpler ones.

ABOVE: *A pair of exquisite seventeenth century red velvet mittens with satin cuffs richly decorated with silver, silver-gilt and pure silk threads.*

As metal thread work is a slow, time-consuming technique, the beginner is too often tempted to fill large areas with metalized leather or kid which can never give the same effect of movement as laid thread. Leather certainly has its uses, but should be kept to small areas, or be well-broken by threads or manipulation such as pleating and shaping, padding and decoratively cutting.

Techniques

Couching is the method of securing laid threads to the surface of a background fabric by using a second thread

To begin couching, make a knot in the working thread, run it through the beeswax, and then bring it up through the background to the right side. Leave about

2in (5cm) of the metal thread loose; this will be taken through to the back of the work later. Begin to couch by taking small stitches over the metal thread at right angles to it. These should be evenly spaced and at about 2/10in (5mm) intervals. To keep the tension on the laid thread take a back stitch on the line where the metal thread will cover it, after every fifth or sixth couching stitch. Keep a fairly short couching thread.

The working thread is finished off on the back, leaving 2in (5cm) of the metal thread on the right side. The two ends of the metal thread may now be taken through to the back by using either a large chenille needle, or a sling for a thick thread. To finish with a sling, thread a chenille needle with a length of coton perlé No. 5. Make a hole with a stiletto at the desired spot. Bring the chenille needle up from the back to the right side, leaving the two ends of thread at the back. Take the needle down into the same hole, leaving a large double loop of coton perlé. Place the end of the metal thread or cord through the loop, leaving a free length of thread or cord between the last couching stitch and the coton perlé loop. Then tighten the loop from below, and with a sharp jerk take it through to the back, carrying the metal thread with it. To finish off, unwind the metal thread on the back to separate the fibres. Spread them out and backstitch them to the backing. This prevents any unsightly lump showing on

the right side. When couching, the metal thread needs to be held firmly and very slightly pulled to keep it taut. At the same time it should be turned to tighten its own twist. This is especially important with Jap gold, as otherwise the orange thread core will show between the gold. Metal threads may be couched singly, or in pairs, for which a very fine thread is used. The couching stitches can form their own design over the laid threads (lozenges, scrolls or squares) as seen in pieces of *opus anglicanum*.

The simplest designs are those where the couching stitches form straight lines or a *bricking pattern*. Threads may change direction leaving a gap between them to show the background colour, or be filled with a textured filling. When laying double threads at a right angle, take a separate stitch over each thread in the angle, to ensure a good sharp turn. Tweezers can be used to help turn the thread. When turning an acute angle and filling the space with couching, lay the outer thread round the angle: all the inside threads have to be cut and taken through to the back as they reach the angle, forming a dovetail pattern.

When working solid areas of couching the threads often have to be turned back on themselves with no background showing. A single thread turns quite easily with a stitch on the turning point, and a stitch over the double thread to hold them together before resuming the normal couching pattern.

Simple couching is a reasonably quick way to fill large areas. Begin by placing metal threads in a vertical line and securing the end to the wrong side. Using a fine couching thread, make the first stitch across the end of the laid threads (**1**). Make evenly spaced couching stitches to end of row, turn metal thread on surface placing it next to previous row (**2**). Continue to couch making a 'brick' pattern (**3**).

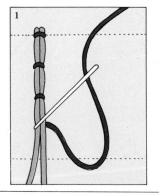 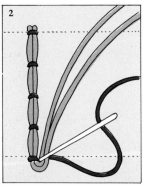 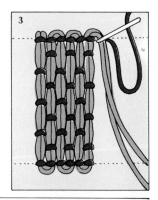

Basketwork: this form of padded metal threadwork has a basketweave appearance. First cut lengths of string to size and place them evenly in the opposite direction to which metal thread will be worked. Couch down with fine thread, securing ends firmly (**1**). Using two strands of metal thread, take it over two strings and tie down with a single stitch (**2**). For next and every other row make the first couching stitch over one string (**3**).

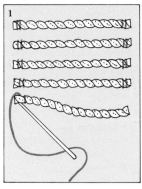 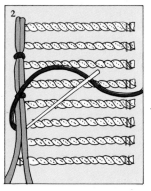 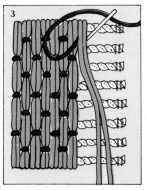

MATERIALS

A frame must be used, as both hands are required to handle the threads. The background fabric and backing should be at a firm tension, but not drum-tight, as this can cause problems if the embroidery is to be free-hanging on completion.

Backings should be closely woven cotton fabric.

Backgrounds can be of almost any type, weight or finish. It is difficult to work metal thread well on a heavily textured fabric, but the embroidery can be worked onto a smoother fabric and then applied onto the selected background.

Needles crewel needles, sizes 8-10, are suitable for most metal thread work. A large chenille needle is used for taking metal threads through to the wrong side.

A stiletto is useful for making a hole to take the larger threads through to the back.

Scissors with short, strong, straight blades are needed to cut the wires.

Tweezers help with handling short lengths of purls, wire or beads.

Sewing threads Since the disappearance of Maltese silk, a matching twisted sewing silk or embroidery thread is the best for couching metal threads. An invisible thread gives good results but is difficult to handle.

Beeswax protects the sewing thread. It also helps to prevent knotting.

Metal threads can be bought in a wide range of shades of gold, silver, aluminium and copper, but the antique colours and more subtle tones and textures take some finding. Even then one must be prepared to make one's own twisted or finger cords in the unusual shades, as only very fine threads are available. Jap gold and silver have a core of threads round which is wrapped a fine covering of metal. Imitation silver-gilt is only now available. Purls are coiled wires of different size and texture which are cut into short lengths and sewn down like beads. Pearl purl, a heavier coiled wire, is couched down as a continuous length, which is slightly pulled out to give it stability. Crinkle, passing, tambour and twist are some of the wide choice of imitation gold threads. Cord and braids are made in different sizes and patterns, both real and imitation. Metallic coloured yarns are also widely available.

Felt covered board approximately 6 x 4 inches (15 cm x 10 cm) helps to control the purls when they are being cut.

Felt, of a near-matching colour, is used for padding.

String, dyed with a waterproof ink to match the thread, is used for padding and fillings. It should be smooth and tightly twisted.

BOTTOM *reels and skeins of thread showing passing thread, jap gold and lurex threads which can be used for machining. In the foreground small reels of Maltese silk used for couching down threads.*

Silver passing thread

Smooth silver purl

No10 silver twist

Thick silver rococo

Rough silver purl

Thin gold rococo

Smooth gold purl

Gold check purl

No1 gold pearl purl

No10 gold twist

No 3 gold pearl purl

8-ply gold lurex

With a double thread take the inner one back on itself first and secure it with a couching stitch, then couch the outer one separately on the turn. Resume normal couching on the straight run.

There are a number of methods of padding a shape to raise it, including the use of felt padding as in stump-work, or padding with card.

Or nué is a development of couching, using a coloured thread to give areas of solid colour and depth. A fine couching thread must be used, or the laid threads may be forced apart. The laid threads are covered by the coloured threads.

There are many techniques for adding decorations to the surface of metal thread embroidery. Purls are pieces of tightly coiled wire, with many variations of size and texture; they are cut to length with nail scissors, threaded on to a needle and used like beads. They are easy to handle, but practice is needed to cut them accurately for geometric patterns and fillings. They are rarely used at more than ½in (13mm) short, lengths. Pearl purl is a heavier coiled wire, which is couched down as a length. It should be slightly pulled out to give it stability, and to allow the couching thread to slip down invisibly, between the coils. With the aid of tweezers it can follow a line accurately and give very sharp corners, which add bite to a design. The cut ends are left on the surface of the

right side, turning the ends under to prevent catching.

Twisted cords are sewn down with a slanting couching stitch, which should lie within the twist so that it cannot be seen. On small cords, the couching stitch is taken right over, but for a thicker cord the stitch is taken into the twist, from alternate sides of the cord. The ends are taken through to the back with a sling. Russia braid and some other flat trimmings are sewn down the centre with a small straight stitch.

Leather is usually applied over padding, and held in place with a suitable light adhesive, or by tacking stitches. These should be carried right over the leather to avoid making more holes than necessary. Sew the edges down with small straight stitches, working up through the background fabric, just under the edge of the leather, then down through the leather. This curls the cut edge under. Leather can be used to cover a piping cord; cut a strip just narrower than the diameter of the cord. Lace the two edges together, stretching the leather into a smooth, tight covering, and sew on near the lacing line from alternate sides. To quilt leather over cord, first stitch it down to the background, down the line where one edge of the cord will lie. Push in the cord hard against this line, stretch the leather over it, and stitch into position. To manipulate leather into sculptured shapes, begin with a piece much larger than finally required.

Circular couching: begin by folding metal thread in half. Bring out couching thread on edge of traced circle, pass needle through loop and reinsert at starting point (**1**). Bring needle out on straight line and couch with a small stitch (**2**). Bring needle out on next straight line (**3**) and couch in a similar way (**4**). Continue couching in this way until the circle is filled (**5**). Keep stitches on straight lines (**6**). Neaten threads on wrong side (**7**).

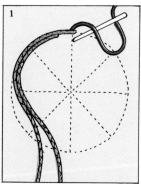
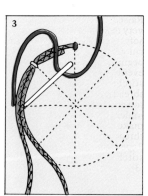
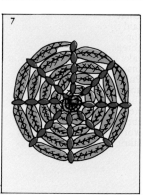
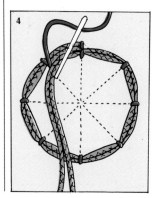
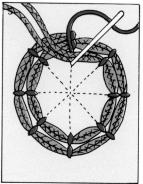
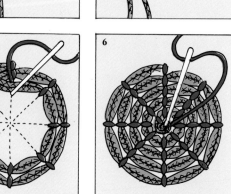

Padding with card: small, individual padded motifs can be made using thin cardboard cut to a simple shape. Attach card to ground fabric with one or two stitches at each side (**1**). Secure end of metal thread to wrong side and continue couching up to the card (**2**). Take metal threads over card, hold down with small stitch at edge taken into same hole. Complete the couching (**3**).

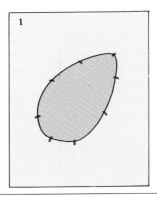
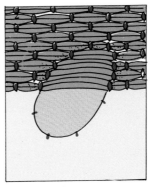
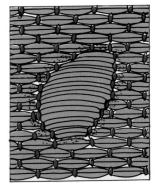

Knotted buttonhole stitch is a pretty feathery stitch useful for sewing jewels and spangles to ground fabric. Bring needle out and take thread once around finger (**1**). Transfer loop from finger to needle and make a buttonhole stitch in fabric (**2**). Continue with evenly spaced stitches (**3**).

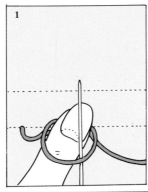
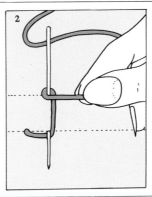
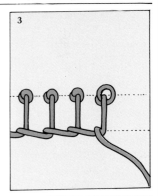

Raised chain band can be very decorative worked in soft, metallic threads in two colours. Working downwards, begin by making a series of evenly spaced horizontal stitches (**1**). Using a contrast thread, bring needle out at top and take it over and under the first stitch. Then make a loop stitch with thread under needle (**2**). Repeat on each horizontal stitch to complete the band (**3**).

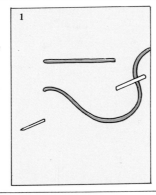
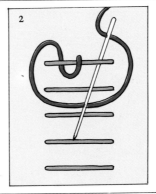
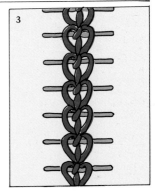

Underside couching: secure laid thread on wrong side at top left. Bring couching thread out a little below, take it round laid thread and insert into same hole (**1**). Pull firmly taking a small amount of laid thread through to wrong side (**2**). Keep an even tension throughout. Continue to work like this covering the fabric surface as needed (**3**).

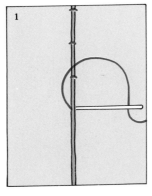
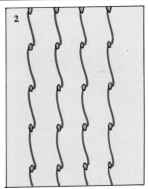
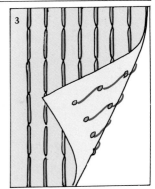

LEFT: *This elaborately embroidered eighteenth century English dress is worked in coloured silks and silver thread on a cream silk fabric. The top of the skirt is supported by padding which displays the embroidery in all its beauty. The hem of the skirt is covered with a band of scrolling shapes worked in couched silver thread which in some areas is worked over padding. The metal thread is also used for the stems and some of the leaves, and adds richness to the multicoloured silks. The floral design is typical of the period and includes roses, peonies, lilies and carnations. Most of the silk embroidery is in long and short stitch and the smoothness of this contrasts with the couched and padded metal thread.*

RIGHT: *The panel shows the Ox, symbol of the Evangelist, St. Luke. Using the traditional or nué technique, the panel was worked from the top. A double gold passing thread was couched down with coloured silks following a design previously painted with water colours on the linen background. Transparent nylon thread was used to couch the spaces between the coloured silks.*

Sew down one edge to the side of the shape, pulling the leather towards you; allow some ease in the width. Pin down and stitch. Work in small areas, having ease in one direction and tension at right angles to it.

Seeding can be used to add depth and texture to an area. All weights of thread can be used for French or bullion knots. Beads, spangles and glass tubes can all be used for a change of texture, but too much glitter can detract from the subtlety of the laid threads. Sequins and spangles can be held on with cut purl, a bead, metallic thread, and used singly or in groups. Beads can be strung together to cover a raised shape, or used to fill shapes; glass tubes and large bugle beads can be couched with purl or embroidery threads singly or in lines.

Gem stones are often difficult to apply, especially if they do not have drilled stitching holes. A metallic thread may be used to work knotted buttonhole around the base, building up a setting that grips the stone. If a stone has holes for securing, a setting can be worked around it using purls, threads or beads. Plate is a shiny, flat metallic band. It is most effective when given a texture, by crimping over a screw, folding in different directions, or couched with a contrasting texture, such as purl. The sharp end must be folded underneath and stitched down. Metallic paillettes can also be used to give sparkle.

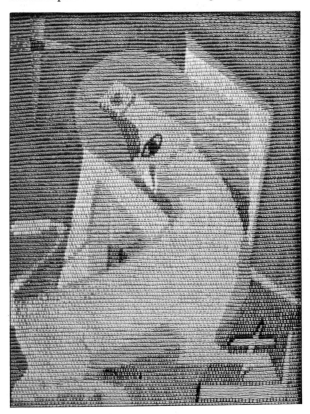

EMBROIDERY FOR CHURCHES

Much of the best metal thread work of the past has been made for use in churches; vestments, altar-cloths, banners and so on. When designing for ecclesiastical work, remember that during a service there is a captive audience, who have a long time to see and consider the work and its meaning, but often at a fixed distance. Symbols should be easily discernible, the design should be clearly understood, and above all there must be movement within the design, so that the eye can flow happily over it. This movement will give food for thought and serve to represent a living faith.

The great difference when working ecclesiastical embroidery after working domestic objects is the change of scale in both design and treatment. The whole has to read at a very great distance, and yet still exel in technique and detail when studied at close quarters. Consequently, you should not rely on variation in weight of the threads and cords, or the contrasting lay of the threads, to give the necessary tonal variation to make the work read at a distance. Take full advantage of the range of shades available in threads, cords and leathers. The brightness of metal threads and cords can be brought out by laying dark cords alongside or among them, giving an accent to the finished texture. The *or nué* technique, with its subtlety of colour, and more important, variation in tone, can be used to great advantage. Try padding and raising important areas; this creates real shadows, which can be of the greatest value.

Take care that vestments are not so weighted with embroidery that they become stiff and uncomfortable to wear; and that none of the materials or techniques you use will catch, rub, pull threads or otherwise become unsightly with regular use.

This detail from a contemporary altar frontal at Salisbury Cathedral shows a chalice design based on a medieval chalice discovered in 1980 within a tomb that was opened up for repair. It is worked in or nué *technique on gold kid leather that is heavily padded with felt to the depth of 1½-2in (3.7-5cm). The* or nué *is worked in coloured silk threads. The chalice is encircled by the crown of thorns.*

SEQUINS, BEADS AND SHISHA

Sequins

Sequins, or spangles, are small flat discs of shiny plastic material used to add brilliance and glitter to fabrics or embroidery. They are available in metallic finishes, gold, silver, brass or copper, and in a wide range of colours including black and white; pearly and iridescent finishes are also made. They are usually round with a central hole for sewing down, although other shapes, for example stars, flowers, leaves and ovals, are available. Paillettes are usually larger than sequins and have two holes for stitching down. Sequins have been used in embroideries for many centuries.

Beads

Like sequins, beads are often used in conjunction with embroidery to add highlights and colourful patterns. Beads can be used singly or in clusters — to decorate the whole surface of a garment, for example — where the facets of the many tiny beads add sparkle, colour and weight.

Shisha work

This type of embroidery involves stitching small pieces of mirror glass or mica to fabric with embroidery stitches. The technique was used originally in parts of India and Pakistan and is now used in many areas of the West.

RIGHT: *This detail of the lower part of a 1920s Parisian dress shows intricate beadwork on a net ground. Tiny mixed coloured beads form a deep fringe below a ribbon which divides different styles of beadwork. Paillettes, bugles and rocailles have been stitched with contrasting colours into a floral pattern.*

Single back stitch is used for attaching sequins singly or in rows. The back stitch tends to tilt the sequin which gives a sharp contrast to the sparkle. Using matching coloured thread, bring needle out and thread on a sequin. Make a back stitch over right side of sequin and bring needle out to left ready to thread on next sequin. Place sequins with edges touching.

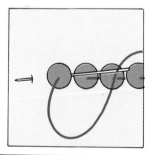

Back stitch Thread on a sequin and make a back stitch to right bringing needle out close to left side of sequin. Make a second back stitch through eye of sequin and bring needle out to far left, as shown in diagram. Back stitch the next and subsequent sequins placing the edge close to the previous one.

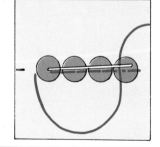

Invisible sequin stitch Using matching thread, bring needle out and thread on first sequin. Place on fabric and insert needle to left close to edge of sequin and bring out the same distance to left. Thread on second sequin and make a stitch over left side of first sequin and bring out to left. Place sequin over the eye of the first sequin and continue to row end.

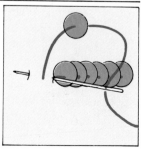

Sequin and bead Choose matching or contrasting coloured beads slightly smaller than the sequins Bring needle out through eye of sequin. Thread on a small bead and pass needle back through sequin. Pull thread tight so that the bead rests firmly in the middle of the sequin to keep it in place. Bring needle out ready for next sequin.

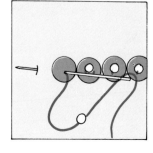

Stitching single beads Useful for attaching beads singly or in clusters. Bring needle out and thread on bead. Insert needle back through the same hole and make a stitch to left slightly longer than the bead, and bring through with thread below needle. Alternatively, make the stitch the same length as the bead so that the beads will touch each other.

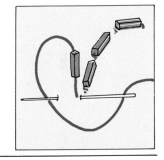

Couching beads Secure the first thread, bring needle out and thread on required number of beads. Slide first bead in place, and with a separate needle and thread, make the first stitch close to the bead. Slide second bead close to first and couch as before, encircling the thread as shown. Complete couching in this way.

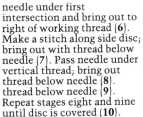

Using a tambour hook Beads can be tamboured onto the fabric in single rows or close together as a filling. Trace the design onto the wrong side of the fabric and stretch it in a frame right side down. Secure a long thread to wrong side, take needle through to right side and thread on a sufficient number of beads. Holding the beads underneath, insert a fine tambour hook or crochet hook a bead length away and pull thread through to form a loop. Slip the next bead along, and with the loop on the hook, insert it after the next bead and pull through another loop. Draw the second loop through the first to form a chain stitch. Continue in this way stitching along the traced line turning the frame to stitch in a continuous line.

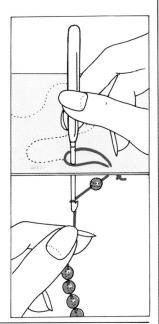

Shisha stitch Hold disc with left thumb and bring needle out at left. Insert at right and bring out above (**1**). Insert at top left and bring out at bottom (**2**). Pass needle under first thread. Pull through and pass under thread above. Insert above disc and bring out to right (**3**). Pass needle under threads as before (**4**). Insert needle below disc and bring out at left of disc (**5**). Pass needle under first intersection and bring out to right of working thread (**6**). Make a stitch along side disc; bring out with thread below needle (**7**). Pass needle under vertical thread; bring out thread below needle (**8**). thread below needle (**9**). Repeat stages eight and nine until disc is covered (**10**).

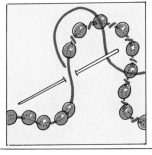

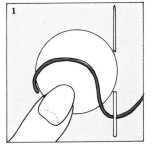

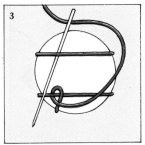

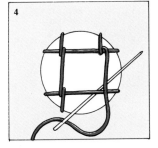

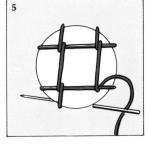

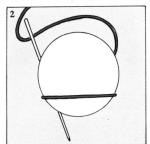

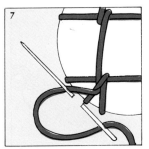

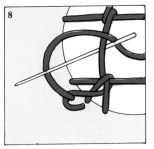

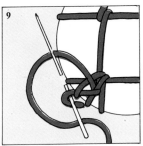

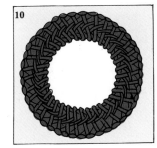

MACHINE EMBROIDERY

Compared with many other embroidery techniques, machine embroidery is a comparative newcomer, although ideas for producing a sewing machine were around as early as 1790. The first machines used a hooked needle and one continuous thread to make a chain stitch, rather like tambour embroidery. Although the sewing machine was developed for practical purposes in the fashion and boot and shoe industries, it was always hoped that it would also embroider. From these early chain stitch machines, more complicated embroidery machines were developed for factory use, notably the Cornely machine.

The domestic sewing machine forms a lock stitch, that is, two threads are used, one from below and one from above. When the tensions are even the stitch is formed in the middle of the fabric, so that the top thread is not seen below and the bottom thread is not seen above. Altering these tensions can produce exciting textures and enables thicker threads to be used in the bobbin.

While the sewing machine's greatest influence was in the fashion industry, from the very start a minority saw its creative potential for embroiderers. One of these was Miss Thompson from the Bromley College of Art, who introduced Mrs Rebecca Crompton (a well-known embroiderer in the Thirties) to Miss Dorothy Benson, who taught in the Singer Workrooms. Gradually the machine became accepted as a creative tool for embroidery, used either on its own or combined with hand stitchery.

ABOVE: *The back of this waistcoat shows machine-quilted lines following patterns painted with fabric paint on polyester cotton, with hand stitched flowers.*

LEFT: *A piece of machine embroidery designed for a fan worked on a domestic sewing machine in about 1900. Solid areas of satin stitch and arabesques of running stitch in delicately coloured silk threads build up this elegant design on painted bolting cloth. Lacy, needle-made fillings are worked in the* spaces, *and the curved edges are finished with tiny picots.*

ABOVE: *This table-centre is a later example of machine embroidery of the mid-twentieth century in which coloured fabrics and nets have been decoratively applied with free machining into a stylized figurative* design. *This is an interesting example of 'drawing' with the machine which became a very popular style of embroidery. A border of formal machine-stitched patterns finishes the table-mat.*

MATERIALS

Sewing machine There are so many good sewing machines on the market today that one is almost spoilt for choice. When choosing a machine for embroidery there are certain factors to be considered. Some machines are becoming so automatic and self-regulating that it is difficult to use them freely. Check whether the feed (or teeth) can be lowered easily — this is usually done by pressing a button. If, instead of lowering the feed, a cover plate is needed to cover the teeth, the distance under the shank is reduced and the needle can catch on the embroidery hoop. Check that the bottom tension can be altered — it needs to be loosened to work whip stitch. In addition to a free arm, see that there is a good sized 'bed' to the machine, which can be easily attached to provide a support for the hoop.
Threads Any fine sewing thread may be used on top. Coats and DMC also produce a fine machine embroidery cotton size 50 and 30 — the latter being the thicker.

Fabrics Most fabrics are suitable except the knitted ones, which would stretch when pulled tight in a hoop. You should also avoid very closely woven cottons, as these can cause the top thread to break.

ABOVE: *A domestic sewing machine suitable for creative embroidery.*

BELOW; RIGHT: *Different machine feet and needles for different types of stitching.*

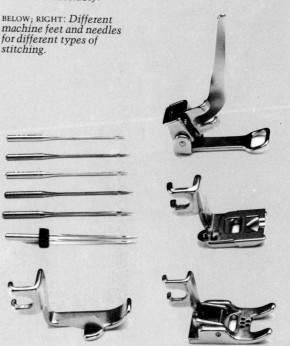

Techniques

Before starting to embroider, check that the top and bottom tensions are even. The bottom tension is regulated by the small screw on the bobbin case and for normal stitching should be neither too loose nor too tight.

Remove the bobbin case from the machine and try pulling the thread, there should be a very slight feeling of resistance. Once you can recognize this feeling, it is a simple matter to return the tension back to normal after it has been altered. An alternative is to buy a separate bobbin case for embroidery use.

Begin by using the machine as if for dress-making, that is with the pressure foot on and the feed working as normal. To avoid puckering, work over paper.

Points to remember: If the bottom tension is loosened the bottom thread will be pulled through to the surface. If the upper thread is loosened the top thread will be pulled through to the underside. While experimenting use different coloured threads top and bottom so that it can easily be seen from where the thread is coming. Try altering the stitch length for different effects.

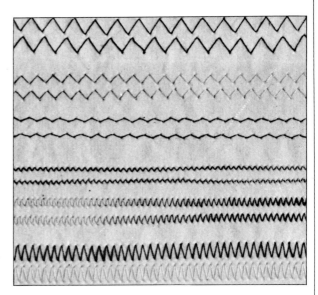

ABOVE: *Basic stitches made on the sewing machine can be altered by using the* pressure foot and changing the length of the stitch and the width of the zigzag.

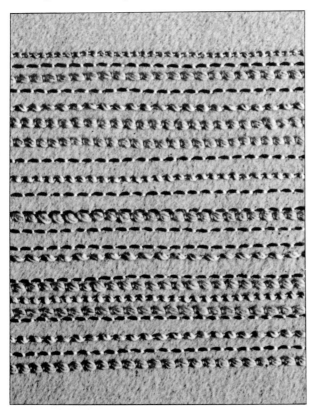

ABOVE: *A thicker thread is wound on the bobbin and worked from the wrong side* with the pressure foot on. The length of the stitch is changed to vary the effect.

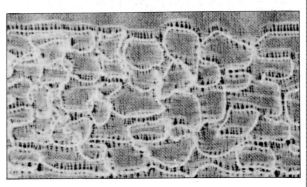

ABOVE: *Pulled work can be worked relatively quickly on the sewing machine. Work on a loosely woven fabric such as muslin in an embroidery hoop using zigzag stitch and both* tensions fairly tight. The example (centre) shows a narrow stitch worked evenly, creating a pattern between the lines of stitching. The stitch size is changed to give a freer effect (below)

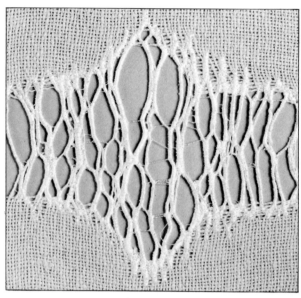

LEFT: *Drawn thread uses zigzag stitch to whip the loose warp threads together after removing the weft threads.*

BELOW: *The edges of tucks are zigzagged and then caught together to give the appearance of mock smocking.*

MACHINE EMBROIDERY

To work simple shapes and gentle curves in machine cutwork, keep the pressure foot on and raise the feed. Machine round the shapes and cut out where required, then machine round the shapes again with short zigzag stitch. Take care when turning a corner by reducing the zigzag to zero.

The small shoulder bag is made in silk noile stitched in a matching coloured thread. The design on the flap is based on water-lily leaves with cut space between the leaves.

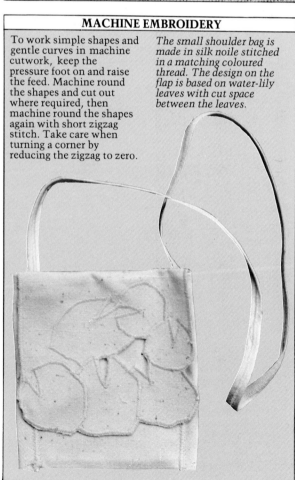

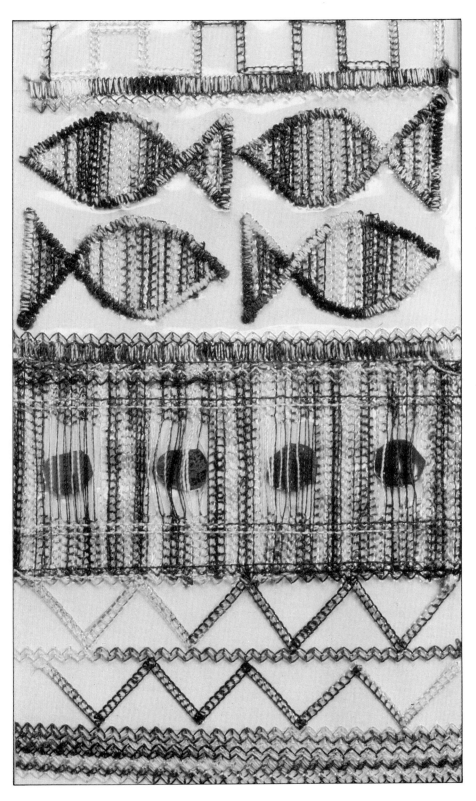

LEFT: *This small experimental panel is worked on transparent acetate using a multi-coloured, rayon machine-embroidery thread. The variety of stitches used make interesting patterns and shapes which appear as silhouettes on the acetate. Zigzag stitch is used in several ways, including closely worked satin stitch — which shows the multi-coloured thread in its full effect. Some sewing machines have a number of simple embroidery stitches from which decorative patterns and border designs can be made — a few are incorporated in this piece. Some sewing machines also have the facility for making extra long stitches which are used to make an interesting contrast to the more densely stitched areas. Pieces of shisha glass are inserted behind these long free stitches.*

Free machine embroidery

When machining with the pressure foot in place, although many interesting effects can be made, you are restricted to straight lines; by removing the pressure foot and lowering the feed, this restriction is removed and the fabric can be moved in any direction. Because the feed is lowered, the stitch length will no longer be regulated by the stitch length setting.

To prepare the fabric stretch it in a narrow embroidery hoop with a screw which takes a screwdriver. To begin with the hoop should not be larger than eight inches (20cm).

The success and pleasure in free machining depends upon the way the fabric is framed in the hoop. The fabric should be larger than the hoop, and stretched very tightly until like a drum, pulling across the grain of the fabric, stretching and tightening alternately (this is where a screwdriver is needed). If the fabric is not too tight, it will flap about and cause missed and broken stitches. Place the stretched hoop under the needle, with the fabric sitting on the bed of the machine.

Techniques

Remove the pressure foot. Lower (or cover) the feed. Thread the machine with machine embroidery or sewing thread. Set the zigzag to zero so that stitching starts with a straight stitch. Do not forget to lower the pressure bar otherwise there will be no top tension, and the thread will tangle underneath. Draw up the bottom thread so that both threads lie on the surface. Holding both threads, run the machine for a few stitches after which both threads can be cut. Hold the hoop on each side to guide it.

Whip Stitch When the bottom tension is loosened, the bottom thread will be pulled through to the surface and wrap around the top thread.

Cable Stitch Thick thread is worked from the wrong side and cannot be threaded through the needle, but these thicker threads can be wound onto the bobbin by hand; it may be necessary to loosen the bottom tension. These thicker threads will not be pulled through the fabric but will lie on the underside, being couched down by the top thread; again, try the effect of altering the length and general direction of the stitching.

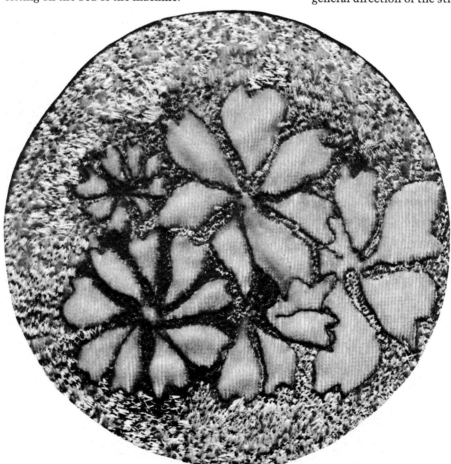

LEFT: *Velvet is used for the background of this example. Free machining is worked to form flower motifs. The petals are outlined leaving the background fabric to show through. Machining on velvet can flatten the pile and will give the work a similar appearance to quilting.*

RIGHT: *This panel uses the sewing machine as a drawing instrument to establish the main lines of the design. Additional texture is built up with dense areas of whipped stitch, made by loosening the bottom tension. The bottom thread is pulled through to the surface and wrapped around the top thread. By altering the length of the stitch very different effects are made. Separate leaves edged with satin stitch have been applied to the background.*

FASTENINGS AND FINISHINGS

Fastenings and finishes are the final touches which can give individuality or style to a piece of work. They combine function with decoration; historically the more elaborate the trimmings, the more status was implied. Tassels, fringes, and cords are used at all levels of society throughout the world. Fringes were originally a functional way of securing the warp ends of weaving; cords were used to lace and tie things together and tassels probably developed from the frayed ends of cords.

In many cultures, finishings have symbolic and religious meanings. Tassels attract the eye by movement, and emphasize gestures in ceremonies and ritual; in some countries they are used to ward off evil spirits. The national costumes of many mid-European countries

make a great feature of cords and braids, which would originally have strengthened pockets, cuffs and collars against wear. Cord was also used to make buttonhole loops and buttons.

On ceremonial occasions standards and banners are considered to be 'undressed' without their tassels; military uniforms are elaborately decorated with braid, the quantity of gold denoting the rank of the wearer. Lacing, which allows expansion and movement, has been used as a way of joining plate armour.

Many of these decorations can be used in present-day clothing and accessories such as embroidered buttons, faggotting or tiny tassels on the ends of ties.

Careful consideration must be given to methods of closing seams and fastenings. Lacings have already been mentioned as a decorative method of closing; laces can be bought or made at home. Clasps are one of the most direct methods of fastening, and are useful for belts and for heavy fabrics. They may be developed from a hook and eye system, toggle or pin and circlet.

Zips are now produced in a number of weights and styles for all types of fabric and positions, but they are still too heavy for delicate or transparent fabrics.

Self-cling tape is another inconspicuous fastening. It consists of two strips, one with a hooked surface, the other tufted, that cling together. It is useful for holding strong fabrics together, and for duvet covers, bags and cushions, where the fixing needs to be closed quickly.

Finishings are as much a part of the design as the embroidery itself, and should be given just as much consideration. Ideally, the finish should be considered from the start as an integral part of the whole concept. It will be governed by the method of embroidery, the function of the piece, and the materials used. Manufacturers allow up to a quarter of production time for finishing; and this is a good rule of thumb for individual projects.

Articles for the home

Many items, such as cushions, curtains, lampshades, and blinds will be seen from two or more sides, or be transparent. This means that hems and turnings should be especially neat, and all ends of threads sewn in. Take care not to overstretch cords or piping. Puckering and distortion are made worse if the cover is either too big or too tight for its pad. Even when correctly filled a rectangular cushion will appear 'waisted', unless its seams curve slightly outwards (this method is not suitable for patchwork or canvaswork), or it incorporates a gusset. Any article for practical use should be constructed from washable, colour-fast fabric.

This chapter gives a broad outline of when, how and where to use particular trimmings, but for more precise instructions, consult a good dressmaking manual.

ABOVE: *A Chinese bag with a pair of very decorative tassels knotted onto a smooth cord end drawstring. The tassel cords are bound with fine metal thread in places and have been formed into a flower-shaped flat knot and then into a second very elaborate flat knot from which three long silk tassels hang. The heads are covered with gold and wrapped with metallic thread.*

LEFT: *An eighteenth-century waistcoat in white linen decorated in self colour with pulled work and corded quilting in a design of flowers and leaves. It is fastened with a row of small buttons made from cloth covered with detached buttonhole stitches. The lining at the back is brought together by smooth cords laced through eyelet holes neatened with buttonhole stitch.*

BELOW: *An Oya-edging of Bibilla lace. This highly coloured lace is used in Eastern Mediterranean countries as a decorative border for clothes, particularly on scarves and head-dresses.*

Seams and edges

The treatment of seams and edges will depend on whether they are to blend into the background or are to become a decorative feature. Many ethnic garments are made up of rectangles and squares pieced together with seams which are joined and often elaborated upon with very rich embroidered patterns of contrasting colours. The fabric for these garments is woven mostly from home-spun linen thread into narrow widths which necessitate piecing together. This embroidery emphasizes the construction of the garment as an integral part of its design. Innumerable variations and combinations of buttonhole and blanket stitches, cretan and herringbone, feather, knot and chain stitches form traditional embroidery patterns which are characteristic of particular regions of the world. Raised chain stitches worked into ladder stitches and closely worked interlaced forms of herringbone can give the appearance of braid. Braids themselves are frequently used to cover and decorate seams and edges. Many embroidery techniques include traditional ways of finishing hems, which are dealt with separately.

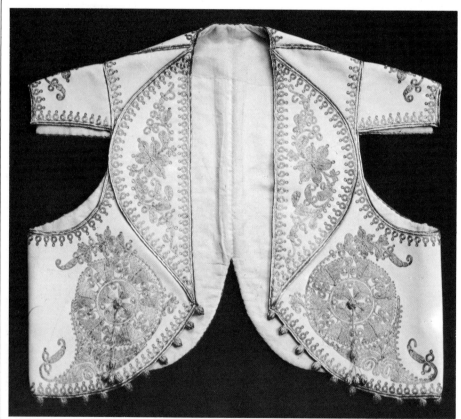

LEFT: *This Turkish waistcoat worked entirely in gold thread on a white ground illustrates the way in which embroidery can emphasize and elaborate upon the constructional design of a garment in both a decorative and functional way. The motifs and borders relate to the curved pieces of the waistcoat which give it its shape. The shoulder seams and epaulettes have been joined and covered with a narrow braid which also neatens all the outer edges of the armholes, epaulettes, neckline and collar, and the shaped hem. This neatened edge is decoratively extended into the cloth of the waistcoat with a border pattern. Buttons, covered with the gold thread and fixed at regular intervals around the hem edge, are purely decorative. The two long elaborate tassels dangling from the symmetrically placed side motifs also display features which move when the garment is worn.*

The restraint on colour in the gold thread on the white ground help exploit the play of light on the gold thread.

Antique faggot hem with diagonal stitches is worked from right to left, making small slanting stitches at each side (**1**).
Antique faggot hem with straight stitches is worked in a similar way to previous stitch, making small straight stitches at each side (**2**).
Half cretan stitch makes a decorative seam. Work a straight stitch across fabric edges and cross with a diagonal stitch (**3**).

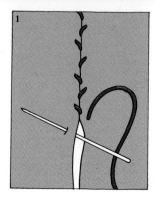
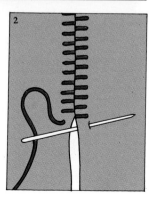
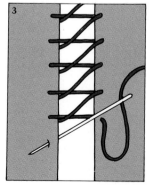

Twisted faggot stitch: insert needle into fabric from behind. Pull through twisting thread in opposite direction ready to make next stitch (**1**).

Buttonhole faggot stitch
Work groups of three buttonhole stitches alternately from edge to edge making centre stitch longer (**2**).

Knotted faggot stitch is worked alternately from edge to edge, making loops knotted in place with buttonhole stitch (**3**).

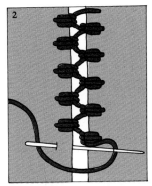
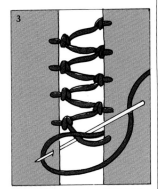
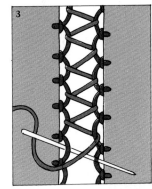

Laced faggot stitch: work from right to left, make evenly spaced loop stitches on edge of fabric. Loop thread, pass needle through loop and behind fabric, bringing needle out with thread below point (**1**). Repeat on opposite side staggering the loops (**2**). Lace loops with a contrast coloured thread, first sewing it to fabric edge (**3**).

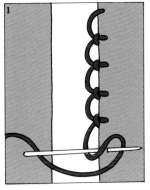
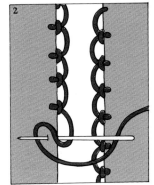
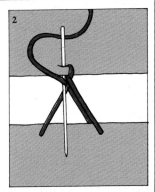

Interlacing faggot stitch: secure thread to bottom edge of fabric, make a vertical stitch on top edge diagonally to right. Bring needle out to left of thread. Repeat on bottom edge (**1**). Take needle up under first thread and insert as before to left of stitch. Bring needle out under thread and over first stitch (**2**). Insert needle upwards at bottom edge, left of previous stitch and bring out over threads (**3**). Pass needle upwards under middle thread, make a vertical stitch to right and bring out with thread under needle (**4**). Pass needle diagonally to left under first and third threads and insert into fabric to left of previous stitch (**5**). Pass needle up under middle thread and insert into fabric as before, bringing it out to left of thread. Pass needle under middle thread and make a diagonal stitch to right. Continue in this way to end (**6**).

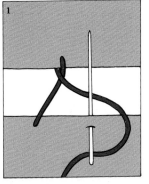

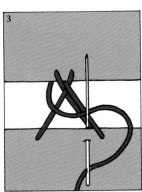
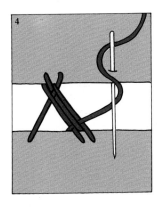
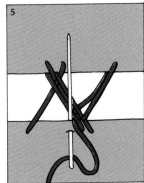
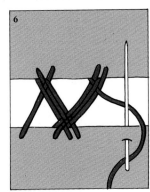

Facings and bindings

Facings can match or contrast, be turned to the front or wrong side, but their shape and grain must match the work exactly. After stitching and trimming the raw edges, notches on the curves and clips at the corners at sufficiently close intervals will ensure a smooth line. On straight edges trimmings can be extended into facings with mitred corners.

Bindings cut on the true bias enable a binding to follow curves readily. They can be of the basic fabric provided it is light, flexible, and not liable to fray. Contrast bindings should be of compatible fibres and dye-fast. Commercial pre-folded cotton and satin bindings are available, but light-coloured ones tend to be transparent and show turnings. Flexible wool- and rayon-plaited types such as soutache are useful. Bindings should be pre-shrunk. Their width should remain even, curves eased smoothly and not skimped, and corners mitred.

LEFT: *An embroidered Spanish collar with a flower design and scalloped edge* *bound in contrasting blue to give a perfectly flat finish.*

Bias binding: to join several strips of bias binding with one seam, first mark diagonal lines on wrong side of fabric and trim off corners. Fold fabric in half on straight grain right sides together. Stitch edges together with one strip extending beyond seam at each side (**1**). Begin at one end cutting around the tube of fabric on marked line to give a continuous bias strip (**2**). To bind an edge (below) stitch two bias strips together as shown (**1**). Press seam open. Fold edges towards middle, right side outside (**2**). Pin binding to main fabric with edges even and right sides together. Stitch along foldline (**3**). Turn binding to wrong side, pin and slip stitch to previous stitching (**4**).

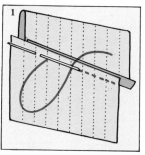
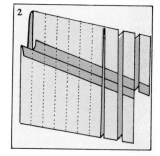

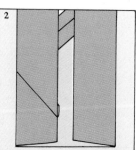
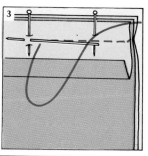
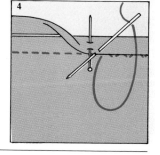

Mitred corners: first make a narrow turning all round edge of fabric. Then fold corners diagonally over to size needed. Trim off corner, as shown (**1**). Fold over one edge, and pin in place (**2**). Fold over second side, pin and stitch across corner with ladder stitch and slip stitch around sides (**3**).

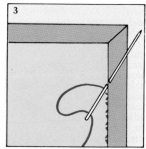

Ladder stitch can be used to join the edges of thick fabrics such as felt or two folded edges. With wrong sides facing, secure thread to one side and insert needle directly opposite. Make an upward vertical stitch through layers (**1**). Repeat on the other side (**2**). Continue to work short horizontal stitches pulling edges close together (**3**).

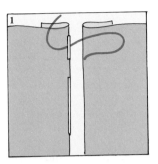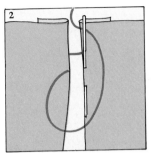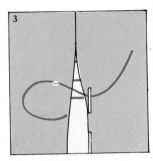

ABOVE: *This spray-dyed and machine-quilted silk bag with its appliqué flowers has been finished with bias binding of the same silk (dyed to a contrasting colour). The binding encloses the raw edges of the inner lining, the quilting wadding and the top fabric and joins the bag together. The bag fastens with a button and rouleau loop.*

Piped edges: piping cord gives a firm finish to an edge. Cut required length of bias strip by circumference of cord plus 1¼ in (3cm). Place cord inside bias strip right side outside, and stitch across close to cord (**1**). Tack piping to right side edge of main fabric matching seamlines, cover with second layer, tack and stitch through (**2**).

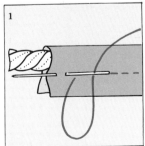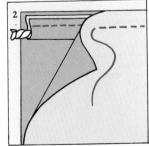

Rouleau: cut bias strips about 1¼ in (3cm) wide and join to get required length by crossing strips right sides together. Trim seam (**1**). Fold lengthways in half right sides together and stitch ¼ in (6mm) from fold, stretching bias slightly (**2**). Do not trim seam allowance or sewing threads. Thread a sewing needle with loose threads, stitch to point of fabric (**3**). Knot the two threads together (**4**). Pass the needle back through the tube of fabric, eye first, working it towards the opposite end (**5**). Gradually turn tubing to right side. Pull on thread and feed seam allowance into tube (**6**) until rouleau is completely turned through.

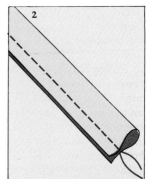

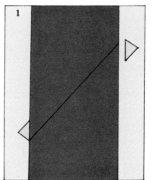

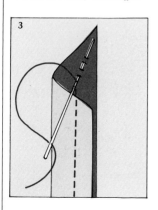

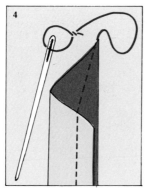

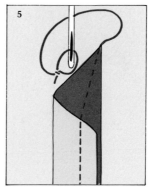

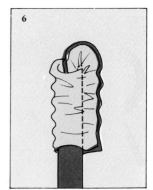

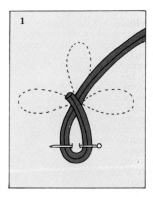

Frogging

This is a bold decorative form of fastening made from spirals of cord or braid, many examples of which can be seen on military uniforms from the Baltic and Hungary. A wide variety of different knot and loop combinations features on European folk costume and textiles from China. The stiffness of the cord or braid affects the way in which they can be coiled and must be designed accordingly. Soft flexible cord such as rouleau can be coiled into tighter, more elaborate frogging. Raw ends can be taken through softly woven fabrics to the back. With firmer fabrics or cords the ends should be tucked under. If the fabric is very stiff flat braids may be preferable.

Method: draw design for frog on paper. Place end of rouleau in middle with seam up, extending end about ¼ in (6mm) (**1**). Pin loops to paper following design and whipstitch through single fabric only (**2**). Trim ends and stitch firmly to hold. Stitches should not show on right side (**3**). Remove from paper and place right side up on fabric with button loop extending over edge. Slip stitch in place (**4**). Make a second frog for button and attach to button side (**5**).

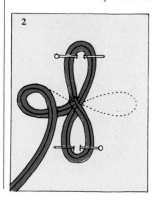

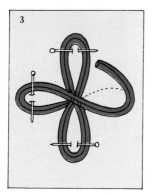

Turk's head knot

The many different variations of Turk's head knots make up a distinctive family of knots which probably take their name from their resemblance to oriental turbans. They are made by lacing cords around in 'over and under' sequences. The basic pattern varies according to the number of crossings made in the centre. Knotted in the hand, the knots become spherical or cylindrical. For larger knots the sequences can be repeated two, three or four times but care must be taken to cross the threads the same way. Using a firm, smooth cord, this method makes an excellent button — particularly if it is used with frogging. Softer buttons can be made from rouleau.

Flat Turk's head knot: working on a flat surface make two overlapping loops from right to left (**1**). Form a third loop to right of first two by passing working thread over the next two threads, under the next two, and over the last (**2**). Make a fourth loop to bottom right by passing thread under and over previous loops as shown (**3**). Insert thread into knot at starting point to make last loop (**4**).

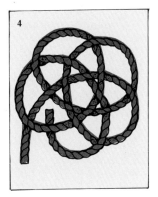

Repeat sequence twice for three-stranded knot. Stitch ends at back.

Cylindrical Turk's head knot: loosely wind thread around three fingers of left hand, slipping first thread over second to form a loop (**1**). Insert working thread through loop from right to left passing it over and under (**2**). Take thread over top of knot passing through first and second threads (**3**). Turn knot round and repeat stage one (**4**). Pass thread through loop from right to left (**5**). Turn knot round. Insert thread into starting point (**6**).

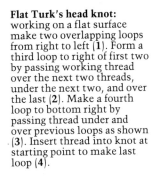

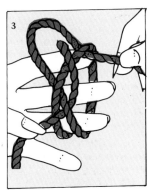

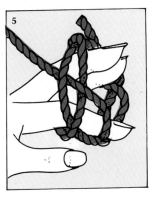

Repeat twice for three-stranded knot.

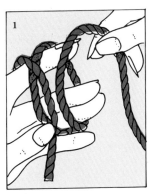

Cords and braids

Cords are round or square in shape and made by either twisting, knotting or looping threads together. Although an excellent variety of decorative cords is available in a full range of colours, they can also be made by hand to match or complement embroidery threads and fabric. They can be used singly, grouped or plaited together. Sometimes beads, shells, sequins and coins are threaded and incorporated into plaited cords to give additional texture and weight. Select the correct cord for the purpose: lace, ties and drawstrings need to be smooth and firm, and knotted or tasselled to prevent them from unravelling and being pulled out of the eyelet. Edging cords may be looped at intervals to make buttonholes.

Braids are flat — either woven or twisted. Many types are available in several widths and textures ranging from russia braid — a soft pliable braid useful for curves and linear decoration, ricrac with its zigzag edges and the multicoloured Greek plait to gold military braids. Some braids fray easily when cut so the ends should be turned under or taken through to the wrong side and the corners eased or mitred.

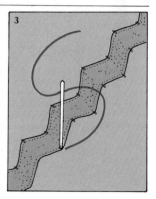

RIGHT: *This beaded American bag, with its softly plaited wool handle in three colours, is notable for the way in which the hole for the cord has been neatened and strengthened by additional bead motifs, to become a very positive decorative feature.*

Hand made cord: cut number of threads required to three times the finished length. Knot the ends to form a loop and insert a pencil at each end (**1**). Ask someone to hold one pencil, and keeping threads pulled firmly, twist pencils in opposite directions until threads twist on themselves (**2**). Holding cord firmly, fold in half and the cords will twist together (**3**). Shake vigorously to keep permanent twist.

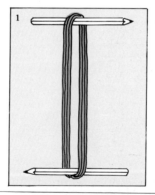

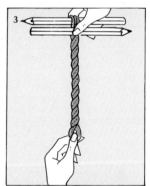

Couching down fine cord: working from left to right, couch cord down with a slanting stitch in direction of twisted cord, picking up fabric under cord only (**1**). **Stitching heavy cord:** make short stitches into both sides of the cord so that they are hidden in the twists of the cord (**2**). **Stitching ricrac braid:** use tiny stab stitches on both inner and outer curves on both sides of the braid (**3**).

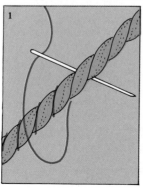
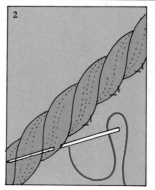
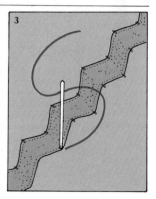

Finger cord: choose a firm thread, and using two colours, begin by knotting the two threads together. Working upwards, make first loop with dark thread and second loop with light thread (**1**). Pull dark thread tight, make next loop, then pull light thread tight (**2**). Continue in this way to complete length needed (**3**).

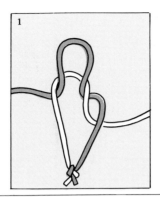
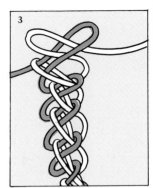
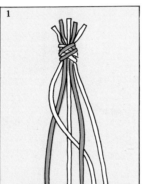
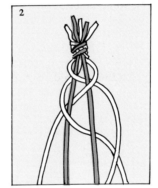

Greek braid: cut five threads — two for the foundation and three for the braiding. Use foundation threads to adjust thickness when stitching down. Knot threads together and secure to work surface. Pass outer thread on left over next two threads to middle (**1**). Pass foundation thread at left over one thread to right and repeat first two stages at oposite side (**2**). Continue in this way to complete the length of braid needed (**3**).

LEFT: *Gold and blue braid has been used to edge the neck and hem of this Yugoslavian waistcoat and lines of russia braid to neaten the armholes. Laid in double and treble bands, the russia braid also forms decorative panels which strengthen the front fastening where purely decorative gold-coloured buttons and loops camouflage strong metal hooks and eyes. On a dark velvet cloth, fine gold cords couched into coiling floral motifs and border patterns exploit the play of light on these gold surfaces. In places sequins have been threaded in with the gold work or held flat with beads to 'spot' the border patterns. This example illustrates an interesting case in which the traditional button and loop fastenings have been superseded by metal hooks, and eyes have been maintained as purely decorative features.*

Buttons

Buttons can be made from a variety of materials including bone, wood, shell, glass, plastics, ceramics and metals of many kinds, and come in all sorts of different shapes, sizes, textures and colours. Used imaginatively, even a single button can become a focal point; rows of tiny buttons, used purely decoratively, and in contrasting colours, may become the main feature of a design. The size of the button should be appropriate for its use, for instance small flat ones on babies' clothing and bolder ones on coats and bags. The character of the button — its colour, texture, shape — can be chosen to match, complement or contrast with the work in a very positive way.

You can make your own buttons by stretching fabric over a button mould. It may be decorated using any of the embroidery methods, and it is often possible to adapt a small motif from the rest of the embroidery. Rolls of fabric or padded balls covered with detached buttonhole stitch make ideal buttons. Washers or curtain rings can be closely buttonholed, or covered in fabric and quilted. Wooden buttons or toggles can be dyed with a 'fibre-reactive' dye to match exactly. After polishing they will withstand normal washing. Of all the forms of fastenings, buttons will be subjected to the most wear and must be firmly stitched on.

ABOVE: *A typical example of a cloth button covered with detached buttonhole stitch.*

ABOVE: *This detail of a button shows a bead covered with gold thread.*

Dorset wheel button: using a metal curtain ring, buttonhole around edge and slip thread through first stitch. Turn looped edge of stitch to inside ring (**1**). Take threads from bottom to top of ring, through south east to north west and so on. Finish with a cross in centre (**2**). With same thread back stitch over each spoke (**3**). Repeat until button is filled (**4**). Finish off on back (**5**).

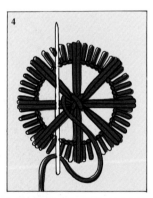

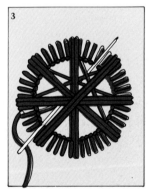

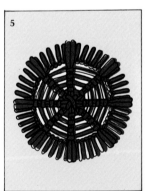

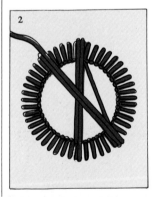

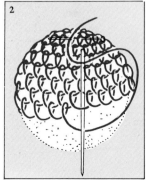

Ball button: shape a small amount of cotton wool into a ball. Pass a straight pin through the top and work two or three back stitches over pin (**1**). Work a row of buttonhole stitches close together around the top, working into the back stitches only. Work more rows below passing needle through loops of previous rows (**2**). Complete stitching, pass needle through button. Remove pin (**3**).

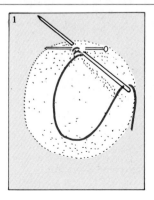

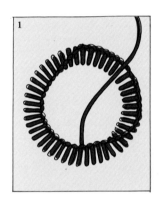

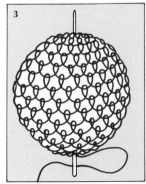

Rolled leather button: cut long triangles of leather to size. Spread adhesive on wrong side (**1**). Cut length of cord needed and place on bottom edge of leather (**2**). Roll tightly finishing with point in middle. Press firmly (**3**). Attach button with cord as preferred.

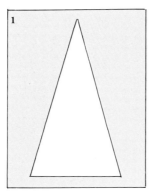
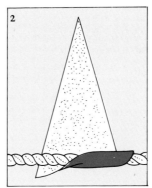
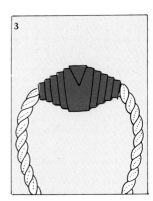

Tassels

Tassels make an ideal finish and can be used in a variety of ways. Tassels attached singly or in clusters can be used as a detail on a box lid, an elegant ornament, or grouped in a mass purely for fun. Any fibre or yarn is suitable. Colours and textures can be mixed for added contrast. Bold tassels can be made from generous bundles of wool, rolled-up pleated fabrics or fringed leather. Long tassels need to be made from fibres that hang well. Although silk is an old favourite it is nowadays quite expensive, but rayon cord makes a good substitute. Beads added to the ends give weight and texture, and tassels made entirely from beads

have an extra quality as they catch the light and are cool to touch. Small, fluffy tassels can be made from wool or chenille, and tiny ones from embroidery threads or unravelled yarn from the ground fabric. Use plenty of material or the result will look insignificant. On the other hand, a tassel should not be too heavy for the fabric into which it is sewn or it will drag it out of shape.

In the past, before commercial fastenings were easily available, tassels were used extensively to finish the ends of ties on clothing. For inspiration, look at the many shapes of metal thread tassels on military uniforms, and civil regalia, as well as those used for interior decoration.

Method 1: cut two pieces of card the length of tassel needed. Wind yarn around (**1**). Tie loops at top with length of yarn threaded onto needle (**2**). Cut yarn between cards to remove tassel (**3**). Bind tassel about ½ in (15mm) from top passing needle through binding to finish (**4**). Leave yarn for attaching tassel.

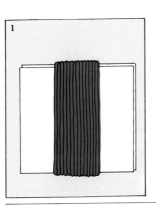

Method 2: bind yarn around card as for tassel above. Thread yarn onto needle and back stitch across top (**1**). Remove tassel by cutting through cards. Knot a length of cord and wrap tassel around knot (**2**). Finish as above.

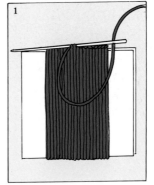
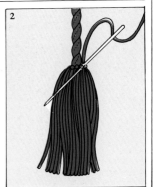

LEFT: *A woman's headdress from Chinese Turkestan. The cap fits tightly to the head and the rich red background fabric is heavily ornamented with silver metal plates, cords and beads. A woven band edges the bottom of the cap, and further decoration is provided by numerous tassels which hang from the crown and sides. The tassels of red and green cords have decorative silver metal heads and each cord is tipped with a silver bead. The weight of the metal and the cords makes the cap very heavy.*

RIGHT: *Four variations of decorative tasselling. Clockwise from top left: a modern bag made in canvaswork and leather with fringed leather tassels finished with buttonholed heads and a hand-made cord of twisted matching perlé thread; a Victorian bag with a patterned-chain design showing the background canvas between. The manufactured drawstring cord and chenille tassels were then to be commonly bought at haberdashers; a hair ornament from a hilltribe in Baluchistan made from chicken bones, beads and hand twisted cords; a canvaswork bag from Baluchistan. Its drawstrings are of hand-made twisted cord and the bag is edged with a beaded fringe and hung with beaded tassels.*

ABOVE: *A canvaswork bag with two simple handles of twisted cord and matching tassels. The same cord has been couched around the entire bag to neaten and finish the edges.*

RIGHT: *A double-sided purse with metal clasp made of beaded net and hung with*

matching tassels made up with a variety of beads.

BOTTOM: *The edge of this cloth has been neatened with closely worked buttonhole stitch which forms the last line of the richly embroidered border which is finished with a section of silk fringing.*

Simple tassel with buttonhole top: make the tassel on card for method one, stage one. Thread yarn onto needle and make a loop around threads in centre (**1**). Pad tassel with a small ball of cotton wool. Secure with looped thread underneath. Slip needle through head to top (**2**). Leave threads to be used for attaching tassel. Work detached buttonhole stitch around the head beginning with stitches worked close together (**3**).

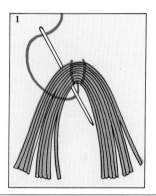

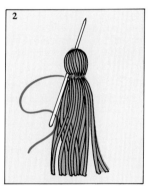

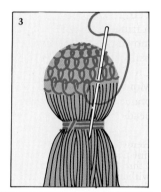

Pompoms: cut two circles of card to size of pompom needed. Cut a small circle in the middle of each disc (**1**). Wind yarn over discs until hole is filled (**2**). Cut through loops between discs (**3**). Ease them apart, and tie a short length of yarn around the middle (**4**) then pull them away (**5**). Leave yarn for attaching pompom.

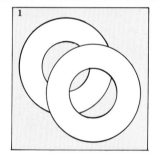

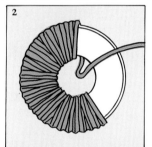

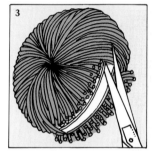

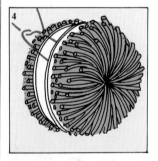

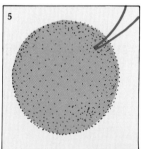

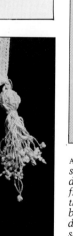

ABOVE: *The heads of the tassels on this white Casalguidi bag are soft balls* covered with detached buttonhole, elaborated with knots.

ABOVE: *These two corded strings of multiple tassels are decorative animal trappings from the East. Each bunch of tassels is secured with blanket stitch, capped with a decorative metal 'head' and separated from the next bunch by a metal tube bead.*

RIGHT: *Notice the Turk's head knot detail on these tassels from a Chinese bag.*

Fringes

A fringe softens an edge and like tassels will emphasize movement. They vary in length, and use. A hemstitched fringe provides a flat edge for fabrics that fray easily. Cross stitch, herringbone or satin stitch can also be used. More unusual fringes can be made from folded tapes or braids (stitched between the edge and facing) or with beads.

Hemstitched fringe: decide finished length and withdraw a thread on this line. Then withdraw two or three more threads only towards edge.

Work hemstitch (1). Remove remaining threads (2).

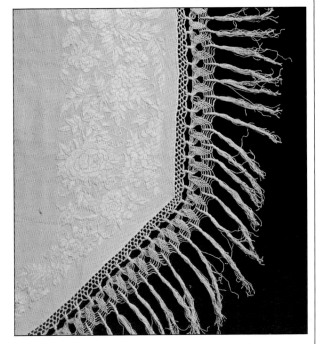

ABOVE: *A fringe looped into a deep band of open stitched edging and then elaborately knotted. The deep fringe brings movement and a silky feel to this white shawl.*

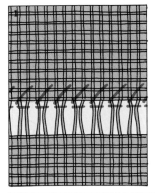 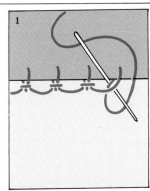

Knot stitch fringe is ideal for fine fabrics with a rolled hem. Work knot stitch by inserting needle into fabric from behind. Bring out with thread below needle, and buttonhole over both threads as shown (1). Pull knot tight, and repeat evenly along edge with loops between. Cut even lengths of yarn for fringing. Insert looped end through knot stitch loop (2). Take loose ends through fringe loop, pull firmly, and repeat (3).

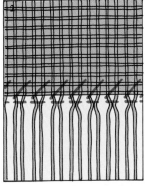 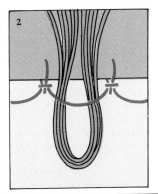 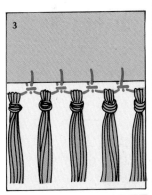

Knotted fringe: first cut lengths of yarn by winding around card cut to size, and cutting across bottom loops. Insert fine crochet hook into seam from underside, and loop fringe into hook (1). Pull ends through loop (2). Knot firmly and repeat along edge (3). Trim fringe ends if needed.

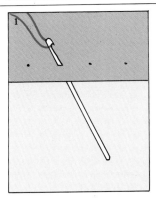 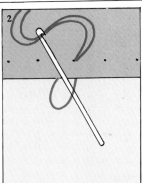 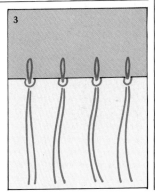

THEMES AND DEVELOPMENTS

Embroidery today encompasses more than the many techniques associated with fabric and thread. By taking a theme, **exploring** its many facets and design possibilities, a very personal and creative approach can be developed. Drawings, natural and man-made objects, photographs, newspaper and magazine cuttings, postcards and other material can all provide starting points for new designs. Collect such things together in a sketch book or notebook, along with scraps of fabric and threads, experimental colour schemes and worked samples and keep them for future reference. Working on one of them over a period can produce a multiplicity of ideas, which can be developed further. One idea will lead to another, and sometimes the result may bear little resemblance to the starting point.

Experimenting with the background fabric brings into use skills other than those traditionally associated with embroidery. Also colour can be added with the use of paints, crayons and dyes. At one time, such techniques were only available to the specialist, but with the wide range of colours and equipment on sale today, this is no longer so.

Cutting and weaving paper together to make a series of new images is a useful way to explore and develop a theme. Cut strips of coloured paper varying in width from 1in (2.6cm) to ½in (1.3cm) and weave them together to produce a rectangular network of pattern. Glossy colour magazines or wrapping papers give some unusual results. Try weaving two separate pictures together, mixing strips of plain colours with detailed textures, or re-arranging and changing the order of the strips.

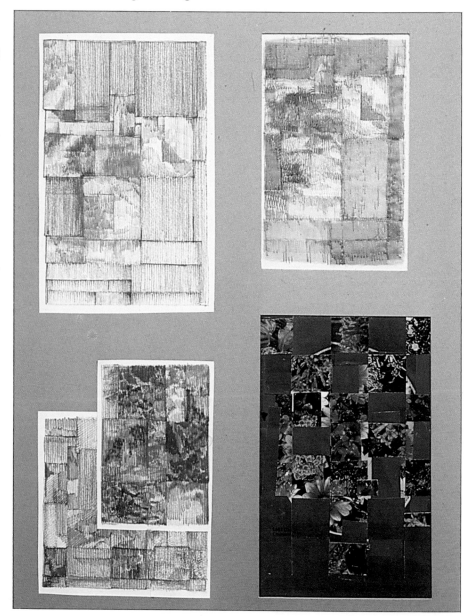

RIGHT: *This example was cut from illustrations in a gardening catalogue, giving a random patterning of fragments of flowers and leaves surrounded by areas of plain green. Use a cardboard viewing frame to select several interesting compositions. Trace the main areas of colour and draw them in with vertical strokes of coloured crayons or pens. These directional lines will help you to translate the composition into close blocks of embroidery stitches. Use thick and thin threads on coloured background fabric, or vertical stitches in shiny and matt threads on a single mesh canvas.*

Fabric strips, cords and ribbons may also be woven together to form a strong structure. Secure by sewing round the edges. Further variations on woven structures may be discovered by consulting books on simple hand weaving.

ABOVE: *Layers of posters have been torn so that the message they convey is no longer important, but intriguingly it is still possible to guess at its content. The fragmented patterns now combine with the texture of the wall, suggesting fascinating shapes and colour combinations.*
Several areas were selected for exploratory colour studies. The embroidery example (bottom right) uses artist's canvas as a background, with fabric crayons, dye, pieces of transparent silk organza and stitches in fine silk threads. Make a collection of pictures of wall surfaces and shop windows with letters and numbers, clothing hanging in your wardrobe or piled on a chair. Use a cardboard viewing frame to help your selection.

ABOVE: *In this design sheet blobs and dashes drawn in water soluble crayons and pencils correspond with the vibrant colours of azaleas. As coloured marks, these lend themselves readily to embroidery stitches. By cutting a drawing into strips and weaving them together, suggestions of garment shapes and patterns made by the new arrangement of marks emerge. Transformations like these provide useful bridges between the original drawing and a satisfying design.*

RIGHT: *The design sheet illustrates examples of Bedouin and Viking ornament (top centre and right). Fabric appliqué is used for two embroidery examples based on the drawing of the bracelets (centre far right). Felt, silver kid and bubble plastic have been cut with pinking shears to give a series of patterned edges (top far right), and a variety of printed fabric strips, cords and hand stitches are used in the bracelets (bottom left).*

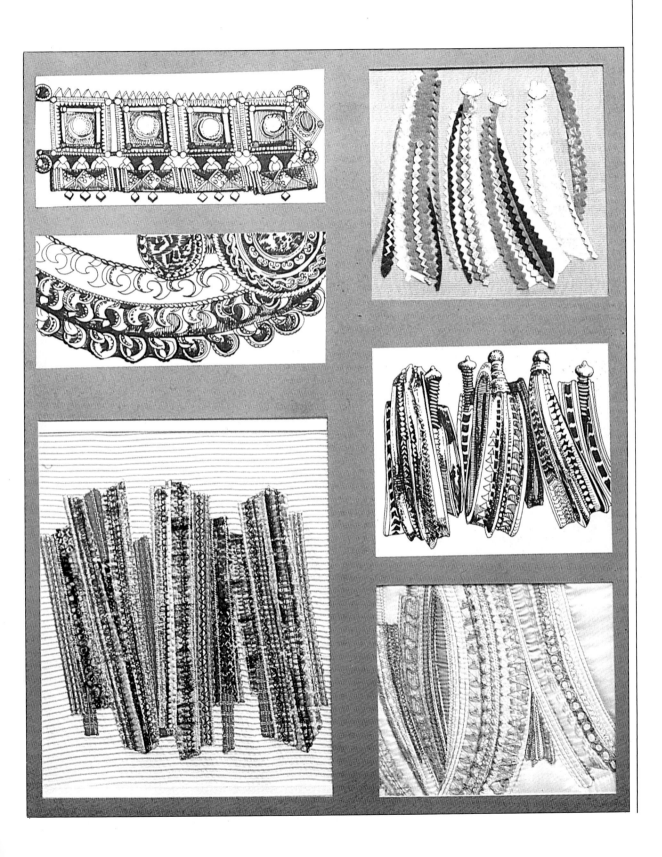

PAINTED TEXTILES

The painted surface can be particularly sympathetic to embroidery, especially when developed with stitchery, appliqué or quilting. The edges of the painted areas can be soft or hard; the colors can blend or be separate; the paint can even be applied in conjunction with the embroidery to develop a design. Most fabrics are suitable as a background and many methods can be used to apply the color such as airbrushing, stippling and spraying as well as crayoning and painting..

MATERIALS

Fabric Paints When colouring fabric for a piece of work that does not need to be washed or cleaned, it is possible to use colouring materials that are used on paper. Paints, crayons, inks and pencils are all suitable, and any of them can be used as long as they do not stiffen the fabric and make it difficult to stitch.

Work that will need to be cleaned requires the use of fabric paints, which are available from suppliers of artist's materials or craft shops. There is an increasing range of fabric paints available. They are always divided into the following groups:

Paints with an acrylic base can be thinned with water or a specific extender and mix very well with one another to create new colours. The colour is fixed with a hot iron when the fabric is dry. Some paints rely on a specific fixer to make them permanent. These are also intermixable. Paints which are dissolved in solvents need only to dry on the fabric to become permanent. These also come with their own extender and brush cleaner. Paints (usually called transfer paints) are applied firstly to paper and then, when dry are transferred to the fabric with a hot iron.

Fabric crayons are also available. They can be used either by drawing or making rubbings on paper and then ironing the image on to the fabric or by applying directly to the fabric.

Fabrics Most fabrics are suitable, for mixed painting methods. The one exception is the transfer paints, which have been formulated specifically for synthetic fabrics. Fabrics need to be prepared by washing to remove any dressing and ironing. Always test the paint on a small piece of the fabric, and explore a variety of fibres and textures. It is easier to work with the fabric stretched flat on a board or a frame.

ABOVE: *Overlapping flower shapes spray-dyed onto cotton through a simple stencil. The design has then been outlined and quilted in matching threads, and the flower centers filled with French knots. The piece has been folded to make the bag, bound together with a bias strip, dyed to contrast and finally fastened with a loop and button covered in detached buttonhole stitch.*

RIGHT: *A fabric paint sprayed with a mouth diffuser onto previously quilted calico. (In this case machine and hand quilting). Spraying from a slight angle catches the padded surfaces to produce this interesting effect. Further hand quilting and stitchery in silk threads have then been worked into the sprayed piece.*

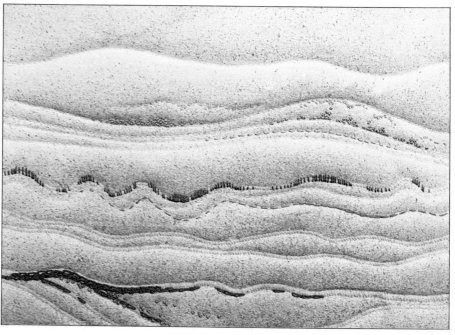

Techniques

Many unusual and interesting effects can be achieved either by applying the colour freely as in a painting or by more precise printing techniques.

Probably the most versatile colours are the acrylic-based paints as these can be thinned with water to give very soft colour washes or used in a thicker creamy consistency for print making. Some of the ways in which the paints can be used are: to brush thin paint onto wet or damp fabric; to spray the paint with a mouth diffuser or air brush, or even spatter with a tooth brush; to cut a stencil and print or spray the colour through the shapes or to explore the marks made by printing with a variety of objects.

The effects that are achieved with the transfer paints rely on the way in which the paint is applied to the paper. This could range from very fine brush work to spraying and spattering. The paint could also be applied to wet or damp paper. It is interesting to experiment with the quality of the paper used, as this can influence the finished result. The colours of the paints are much duller on the paper than when ironed onto the fabric, so it is useful to keep records of the colours on the actual fabrics.

It is important that the fabric colouring integrates with the rest of the work and does not dominate the embroidery. Try exploring the various techniques and keeping samples for reference. By planning the work carefully the painted fabric should enhance the design and the finished piece of embroidery.

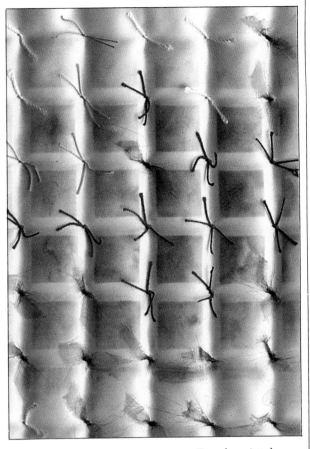

ABOVE: *Transfer paints have been used to create a grid of squares on a synthetic satin fabric, grading from pink to mauve across the design. The squares around the edge of the grid have only been partially transferred by ironing as part of the effect. The painted piece of fabric has then been placed on wadding and quilted with knots tied on top of the fabric in threads of different colours and very thin strips of coloured organzas.*

LEFT: *Fabric paints brushed into damp cotton fabric have been used to create a landscape. More diluted areas of paint and softer tones of colour help to give an illusion of space. The darker edges of painted patches form images of hills and areas of foliage, and brushed streaks suggest weather and light. The addition of simple areas of straight stitches give focus and texture to the design.*

FAR LEFT: *Fabric paints have been used in various ways in this design. The striped, newly mown effect of the lawn was achieved by masking off areas of the fabric with strips of paper or tape and spraying between them in tones of green in two alternate operations. The chequered terrace was printed with a simple block. Notice how effective the characteristically uneven quality of hand block printing is to the whole design. The flower and foliage borders are built up on a painted ground. Tiny scraps of various fabrics have then been applied in a very free textured way and surrounded by different embroidery stitches.*

LEFT: *The cotton fabric has been unevenly sprayed with fabric paint to soften the starkness of a plain background, and giving texture and tone in which to build the design. The images, developed from drawings of plants in plastic seed trays, are suggested with softly painted areas. The frames of the seed trays are cut from thick bonded interfacing and covered with painted fabric before being applied. The flowers and foliage are developed with applied scraps of fabric and free stitchery, which fill and flow out of the geometric shapes.*

MARBLING ON FABRIC

Hand-marbled paper has been used since the fourteenth century in bookbinding. The technique, which is based on the principle of oil floating on water, can be used on fabric; it has recently been enjoying a revival, for wallpapers, and for certain fabrics and upholstery materials. Fabrics to be used must be well washed and ironed beforehand to ensure that they are free of all dressing. They must be smooth-surfaced to allow the inks to bond. The finer the fabric, the better the print: fine cotton, linen, silks and rayon are all suitable.

MATERIALS

Carrageen moss (Irish seaweed) is available from health food shops and chemists. Alternatively, Gelozone, a powdered form, may be used.
Campden tablets (sulphur dioxide) are used for a preservative and are available from home wine-making shops.
You will require oil-based fabric printing inks (sold in tubes) and oil for thinning fabric ink.
You will also need a tray or trough. Old meat tins or plastic cat litter trays are suitable, or photographic trays, though these are relatively expensive.
Small containers for mixing, such as saucers or plastic pots and small sticks for stirring are very useful. An old comb, fork, feathers, knitting needle and straws are useful for making patterns.
The fabric must be rinsed immediately after printing, so work close to a sink.

ABOVE: *A quilted marbled fabric in pinks and greens in which the flowing lines of the design are emphasized by coloured lines of running stitch. The quilting accentuates the shapes and curves and the spaces are filled with beads and French knots.*

BELOW: *A marbled design has been cut vertically into different widths. These have been spaced out to include plain yellow strips and machine-pieced together into alternate stripes. Flowing lines of couched threads are worked across to reinstate the marbled patterns.*

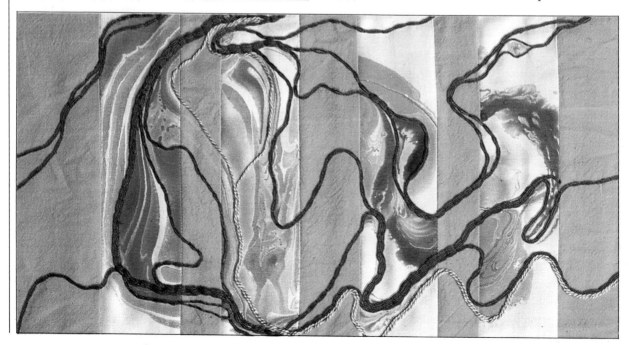

A detail of a design, quilted with running stitch using matching thread to outline the marbled shapes is effective for its simplicity and slightly raised, textured quality.

Techniques

Take 1oz (28gm) of Carrageen moss and add to 3 pints (1.77 litres) of cold water in a large pan. Bring to the boil gradually, and allow to boil for four to five minutes, stirring constantly. Remove from the heat and add 20 fl ozs (0.57 litres) of cold water, and one Campden tablet. Leave for 12 hours or overnight, until the solution sets to a soft jelly-like consistency. Strain through a fine sieve or old stocking.

If using Gelozone, take one level tablespoonful of the powder, shake with a little cold water taken from 2 pints (1.2 litres) to a smooth paste in a pan. Gradually add the remainder of the water to the paste, and bring to the boil slowly; boil for two minutes, stirring continuously. Leave to cool and strain.

Testing It is important to test the solution to make sure it and the pigments are the right consistency. Otherwise results can be variable.

Place the solution in a tray to a depth of approximately 2in (5cm). Mix the inks to a smooth creamy consistency with a little thinner; start with a squeeze of about 1in (2cm) and add thinner a drop at a time. Remember you can add thinner but not remove it. Some pigments require more thinner than others.

When the ink seems to be of the right consistency, take a little on a stick and gently drop a spot into the solution. It should expand and spread a little. If it does not spread, the solution should be thinned with a little water. If the colour spreads and then shrinks, the solution is colder than the inks; add a little warm water.

The aim is to get the solution to the correct viscosity, so that it will hold a pattern long enough to print. After each test, clear the surface by skimming the edge of a piece of newspaper over it.

Printing Gently drop two or three colours on to the surface of the solution. They should spread but not mix. Now create your pattern, by swirling with a comb, fork or feather into a wave pattern, or gently twist into a flower-like motif. Try using a straw to blow the colour over the surface. Take care not to drive the colour through the surface to the bottom of the solution.

When ready, carefully lower the fabric on to the surface of the tray, working from the centre to the edge. It is simplest if the fabric is about the same size as the tray; if working with a large piece of fabric, ask another person to hold corners with you. After a few seconds, lift holding corners, and reverse onto a newspaper, so that the right side is now uppermost. Take to a sink and rinse under cold water; spare ink and solution will run off, but the design should remain clear. Hang up to dry, and when dry set the fabric with a hot iron.

All the colour should have been taken up when the print was taken, but skim the solution with newspaper before printing again.

Do not be disheartened by failure at first. Marbling is an art, and it takes practice to master sufficiently for a precise result. Though it is always difficult to repeat exactly, with practice one can control the colour and pattern sufficiently to produce enough matching pieces to make a dress or waistcoat.

THE PAINT BOX PROJECT

The following examples are taken from an in depth study made under the title 'Boxes of Paints'. An old school paint box and some crumpled tubes of paints in cardboard boxes were the starting points. Drawings were made of these from various angles. Working on one theme over a period produced a multiplicity of ideas: the end results bear only a distant resemblance to the starting point.

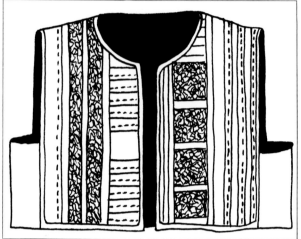

TOP LEFT: *A line drawing of the layout of the paint box.*

Folded, pleated and crumpled tissue paper provided an effective way by which to see how fabric might be used along similar lines (bottom left). The shape and effect of this 'try-out' suggested simple garments. Swatches of fabrics and threads in colour schemes and texture groups can be gathered as useful reference material and worked samples often become another source of inspiration and ideas. In this case variously textured cream silks, laces, and ribbons were collected. Possible waistcoats were visualized and variations for the back and front of a

woman's waistcoat were then designed and tested by simple line drawings (above) — finally the idea emerged: a waistcoat to be built up by applying strips of variously coloured textured cream silks, laces and ribbons to a background fabric with some surface embroidery and insertion stitches incorporated into the design. A rubbing taken from the same paint box gave an interesting texture and design. A tracing was made roughly following the pattern of the rubbing with a continuous line. This was followed by an experiment with free machine quilting. A layer of wadding was tacked between a backing of firm (pre-washed) calico and a top fabric of thin jap silk. This was then free machine-quilted, lowering the feed-dog and using the darning foot, but no frame. This worked well.

The final waistcoat (below) was designed and made. The quilting was worked very freely on the machine using the original rubbing and tracing as a layout guide, working on the same thin jap silk on its backing of firm calico and layer of wadding between. (It is important to remember that any changes of fabrics, stitching or thickness of wadding from those of the original try-out can considerably alter the effect that was initially so successful.)

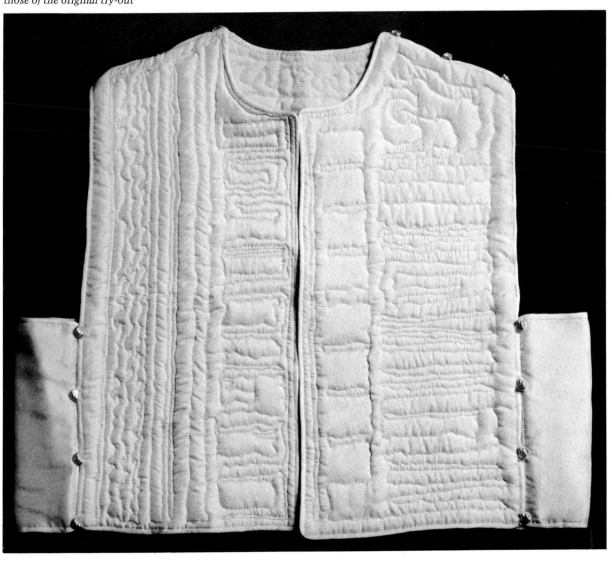

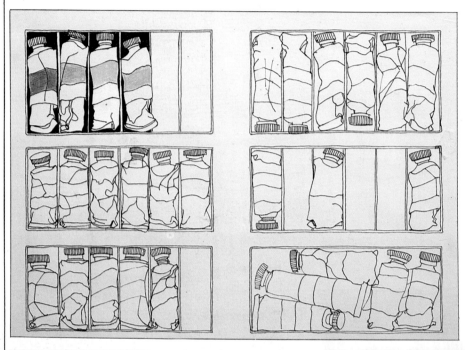

The 'Boxes of Paints' theme was extended to include line drawings of crumpled tubes of paints in their cardboard boxes (left). A number of tracings taken from these drawings were made — some in line, some filled in solidly with colour, some overlapping. (After a while these begin to look like groups of figures — an idea which could be followed up later.)

One of these tracings (bottom left) was then placed in four rectangles and treated in different ways. These in turn could become the basis of further work — as designs for small panels, for example.

A kimono-shaped card 'window' was placed over the last of these (below) and it was decided to go ahead with this idea.

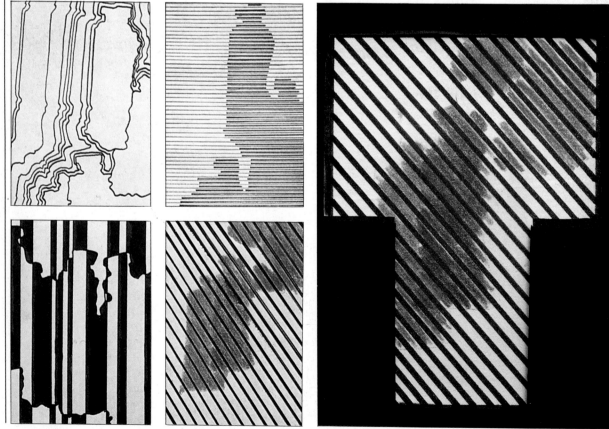

Experiments were made with
fabrics. Thin silk was dyed
and torn into strips, then
machine-stitched down the
centre of each strip to a
cotton lawn background.
This created a furry-textured
striped fabric.

(*Above and right*): Finally a
kimono was designed. The
front of the kimono is made
up in black and white
vertical stripes, and the
design of the back follows
the original drawing closely.

THE SHEEP PROJECT

Working from a personal photograph marks an initial step in selection. A viewfinder made from two L-shaped pieces of card allows one to make further selection across the whole photograph. Interesting ideas can be recorded by small sketches and notes. Some areas may be omitted, rearranged, highlighted or played down to help give more impact to the main image.

Drawn from a photograph (right) the traced line drawings (below) make good basic shapes which can be repeated to produce groups and borders. These can be adapted to suit quilting, cutwork and appliqué. Several separate tracings which explore each of the elements of shape, line, tone and texture provide another useful way of getting to know the subject thoroughly. Tracings from the study of texture have been used in a decorative way — for example in the simple cutwork sample (bottom left).

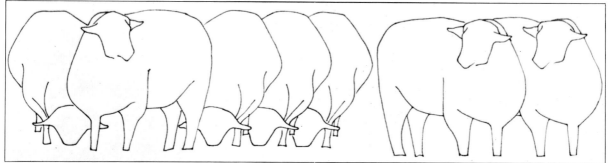

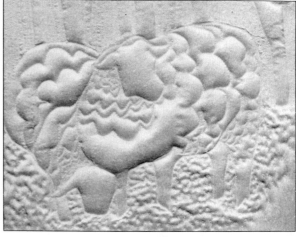

The plain lines of the sheep are outlined with buttonhole stitch, with highlights of satin stitch set against stitched textures which suggest sky and grass. The quilted sample (above) however emphasizes the rounded, curly nature of the sheep and sets them against a background of trees simply outlined.

An interpretation of the
sheep drawn with free
machine embroidery and
textured with hand stitchery
is shown (left). Increased
familiarity with the subject
should encourage freer
interpretations and drawings
using a wider variety of
drawing materials such as
charcoal, pastels, paints and
inks (bottom left). All these
experiments will produce
effects which will then
suggest suitable treatments
in embroidery.
The final piece of
embroidery, (bottom right)
worked on a calico
background, is painted and
machine embroidered.

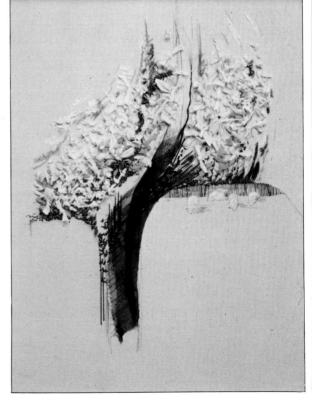

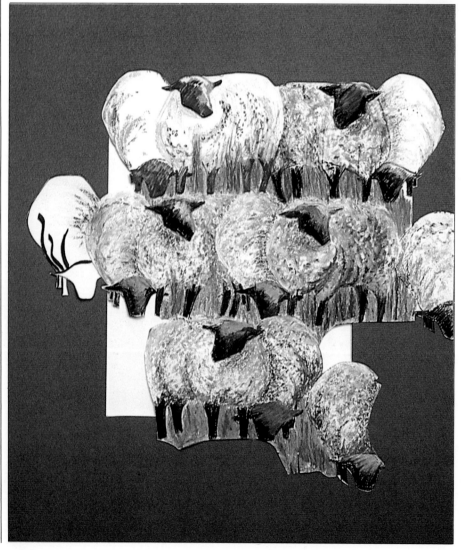

An interpretation of part of the collage design below in fabric and thread (above): the basic shape of the sheep, their black faces and the coloured background have been painted onto fabric and then more extensively developed with free machine embroidery. A collage of paper and paint has been used to extend the repeat image of the sheep previously developed through the multiple tracings from the photograph. The broken edge of the piece has been exploited to give added interest to the design (left)

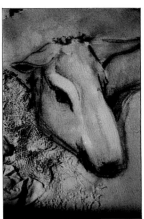

This detail (left) from a mixed media panel shows the group of sheep which have been drawn directly on the calico and worked upon with various paints and colour washes. Scraps of applied fabrics in many different textures have been added. A rich variety of embroidery stitches in many weights and textures has been worked into these, giving a highly textured effect and creating different tonal contrasts.

A satisfactory development may be reached by extending these textural effects and tonal contrasts in an abstract rather than a realistic rendering. This piece (below) begins to explore these possibilities by sewing ribbons, tape and strips of coloured fabric into a grid of painted canvas which is interesting to compare with the machine-embroidered piece.

THE CHERRY TREE PROJECT

The aim of the cherry tree exercise was to capture an atmosphere and create an illusion of space. This involved producing many drawings of the tree seen through a kitchen window. These may have been successful as drawings but were not suitable as such for embroideries. The idea of using collage as a transition between the drawings and the fabric and thread proved to be helpful.

By beginning with the area furthest away — the sky and trees seen through the far side of the cherry tree — and working forward, layer by layer, not only were spatial illusions created but the order in which the embroidery would have to be worked became apparent. Colours that would both recede and 'come forward' were also selected.

When exploring the possible equivalents in fabric and thread, a trayful of samples of fabrics, including silks and laces, and a range of threads were used as a suggested 'palette'.

Studies, colour notes and drawings were made of a tree seen through a kitchen window at different times of the year. This charcoal drawing (above) shows the trees in late winter when the bare branches show the basic structure and spatial form. Glimpses of the surrounding gardens and buildings are seen through the framework of the branches.

This drawing is worked from further in the room and shows the pattern of the branches relating to the window frame and the interior of the room (left). The rich quality of charcoal helps to explore tonal relationships and gives a vigour and spontaneity to the drawing.

In this stage the scale and density of the marks made try to solve the problem of representing spatial relationships on a flat surface. Pieces of cut paper are added on top of the drawing (above left).

The detail of leaves and blossom forms a further analysis and attention is paid to the scene beyond the branches, thus forming another set of patterns (above right).

Paper collages help to interpret the initial drawings and simplify the shapes, colours and tones. A variety of papers including tissue paper are torn and cut to build up the impression of the view

(below left and right). The papers are combined with crayons and paint in an attempt to develop a link between the graphic image and the textile image.

This paper collage (above) explores the transition between drawing and embroidery as a means of creating illusions of space in fabric and thread. Equivalents were then found in fabrics, threads and stitches to the marks made in the initial stages. Tonal values and textures were tested by wrapping a strip of card in colours corresponding with a strip through the collage. Colours and textures which were too strong were used carefully or discarded.

The final result of these studies (right) resulted in a panel where freely applied fragments of fabric, and lace, stem, cretan and straight stitches were worked into a background, softly coloured with fabric crayons, and framed by an appliquéd window blind.

DESIGNING WITH LETTERING

Lettering as a design feature has many interesting possibilities far beyond stereotyped plain letters and dull monograms. Too often letters are included in embroidery as an afterthought, and look dull and misshapen. This is a great pity, as there are so many different styles which can add interest and sparkle to a design. Lettering is a means of communication and as such is seen everywhere in the environment from road signs, posters on hoardings, shop fronts, lorries and graffiti to packaging, newspapers, magazines, record sleeves and television.

The letter forms can reflect the style of a period in the same way as furniture and costume. The flowing sinuous forms of the Art Nouveau period at the turn of the century were evident in the type-faces used; their distinctive decorative style has since been popular again. The Art Deco style which followed in the 1920s and 1930s was a complete contrast, shapes were angular and geometric.

Obviously the style of lettering chosen for a design must be suitable for its purpose. Elegant, finely formed letters such as the classical Roman type may look right for one project, but would be quite wrong for a setting such as a fast food restaurant or disco. Typical examples might be the lettering used on the record sleeve for a string quartet and that chosen for the sleeve of a 'pop' record.

Letters can be used purely as a pattern when legibility is of secondary importance, but if intended to convey a definite message, they must be readable while still retaining their style and balance.

All letters have a height and width. Some are condensed and narrow in shape, others very wide and square. In the alphabet some letters will look very much the same whether drawn as capitals or lower case letters. Serifs give added style; they can become quite exaggerated, which may emphasize their pattern-making qualities. Plain letters are described as 'sans serif'.

The structure of a letter must be considered when using words and phrases, as this affects the spacing. Two straight letters side by side (such as i and l) will need fractionally more space between them than two curved letters to look visually right. However, the spacing between each word is best kept uniform, ideally the width of a letter.

When designing it is sometimes easier to cut letters in paper in the first instance, and move them around until a satisfactory arrangement is reached. Cut paper letters can also be used as templates for the finished design.

When using a number of words or a phrase, it is helpful to see them as blocks rather than individual letters.

In this way it is easier to adjust the balance of the design. When this is achieved the letters can be drawn out properly. Always bear in mind the final working method. A style of lettering which is suitable for fine surface stitchery may be quite wrong for quilting or canvaswork.

The only way to gain confidence in any medium is by practice. Take one letter and draw it again and again in different styles, sometimes small, sometimes large. Make a border pattern by repeating one letter, then take the same letter and repeat it as an all-over design. A design in which the letters touch each other, makes interesting shapes between. Avoid awkward, ugly, contrived ideas, make sure curves flow properly, and if straight lines are used make sure they are *straight*.

LEFT: *A design taking one word and making the letters fit round each other. A variegated stranded cotton is used for the stitching of the letters and the background is quilted with running stitch and couched threads.*

In contrast this panel (right) is designed around a phrase, which conveys a feeling of the enjoyment of a holiday. The letters of the words are deliberately placed up and down to add liveliness. The pennants of the bunting, the stripes of the deckchairs and the ripples of the waves all accentuate this mood. The letters of the word 'seaside' are based on circles and are voided, the stitching round them is denser and worked in a deeper colour. It is a good idea to collect as many different styles of lettering as possible from magazines, newspapers, packaging and brochures.

RIGHT: *This panel is based on impressions of Las Vegas, where a bewildering collection of neon lights flash on and off continuously. Each sign has its own characteristic style of lettering, and the words 'Circus, Circus' in particular reflect the type of letter which is generally associated with fairgrounds.*

The embroidery is in brightly coloured threads on a background of calico. Small circles of silk fabric are applied to the background and the stitching is taken across them. Small straight stitches and some eyelets form a background to the lettering.

BOTTOM RIGHT: *In the exercise on the right the word 'Apple' is designed within a circle and the letters are curved slightly to fit the form. The design is first worked out on paper using coloured pencils to shade the background voiding the letter shapes.*

In the stitched example the different colours of thread are gradually shaded into one another to give the appearance of a rosy apple. The stitching of the background is rows of fine chain stitch in a stranded cotton. Chain stitch is particularly versatile in following the lines of a design.

ABOVE: *The panel (above) is a memory of a visit to California. The cloudless skies and bright sunshine are reflected in the use of colour, and the broken lines of the stitching suggest the shimmering heat. Different types of letters are used for the names, there is a variation in the scale and in the use of capitals and lower case. To give a look of uniformity to the design only* straight stitches are used but in varying sizes and directions. When using lettering in a design it is important to make sure that it plays an integral part. Try to make the letters interesting and lively unless they are for a strictly formal and traditional piece of work.

FELT AND PAPER MAKING

Simple felt making

Felt making is basically a simple process, the only requirements being some fleece, carders, a washing machine and an iron. The following method can be carried out using standard kitchen equipment.

Card the fleece and lay the 'rolags' side by side onto a piece of calico or sheeting. Make a second or third layer, criss crossing the layers each time. More layers can be added if a denser felt is required. It is important to remember that the fleece will shrink considerably when washed, so do not make the initial pieces too small. Lay another piece of calico on top and tack all layers securely together. Make several parcels, place in the washing machine, and wash at 60 degrees in the normal way. At the end of the cycle remove the parcels from the machine and take out the tacking threads. Press with a hot iron, to help shrink and flatten the felt. Remove the calico and allow to dry.

LEFT: *Hand-made felt made into a large hanging with an applied geometric canvaswork motif of stripes and diamonds in dark and light blue, dull pink, white, pale orange and yellow, surrounded by a wide border of white felt and a felted background spotted with pink cotton.*

Simple paper making

Handmade paper is another medium to be explored in the field of embroidery and has many exciting possibilities. It can provide an interesting surface to stitch into and apply as well as to draw and paint upon in the usual sense. Like felt, paper making is quite simple and can be made by recycling discarded paper of all kinds, rags and other cellulose matter. You will need an electric blender, an old saucepan, a mould and a deckle, paper cloths and paper to recycle into pulp.

Techniques

Tear paper into small pieces, add to a saucepan of water, bring them to the boil and simmer for an hour to break down the fibres, then blend the paper into a fine pulp. Fill the sink with water and add the pulp (a fine net over the waste outlet will prevent blocking the pipe). Place a paper cloth on a flat surface nearby. With the deckle on top of the mould and holding them tightly together slide them vertically into the water. Then slip them under the pulp to a horizontal position and lift some of the pulp up out of the water, shake to remove excess water. Lift the deckle from the mould. Lower the mould and pulp face down-wards onto the cloth, press hard and then remove the mould, to leave the sheet of paper on the cloth. With a paper cloth between each sheet several may be stacked together. Press out excess water. Separate the sheets and, attached to their paper cloths, leave the paper to dry.

MATERIALS

To make a mould and deckle make two frames using 1in x 1in (2.5cm x 2.5cm) wood cut into the size of the required sheets of paper. Do not use water soluble glue. For the mould stretch fine wire mesh, nylon or muslin net tightly over one of the frames and secure with staples or tacks around the sides. Seal both frames with paint or varnish.

LEFT: *Many different kinds of paper can be reduced to pulp such as used envelopes and writing paper. Computer print-out paper gives a very high quality pulp whereas pulp from egg boxes is very degraded because it has already been recycled many times. Pulps can be lightened by adding household bleach but remember that this paper will not afterwards take paint or dye. The broken colour print from posters and magazines will give speckled papers. Dyes may be added to colour pulps and very small fragments of fabrics and threads; grasses, straw or leaves will give interesting textures. Handfuls of pulp from the blender or remaining in the sink can be squeezed into 'nuts' and allowed to dry.*
Providing that these have totally dried out they can be stored in trays or jars for future use.

Making a sheet of paper without a deckle on the mould can result in exciting uneven and frayed edges. Dyes added across a wet sheet of pulp or pulps of different colours and textures mixed in the deckle can give interesting colour effects.

When the paper is dry, it can be stitched although it is important to remember that it is not as hardy as fabric. Only fairly simple stitchery should be used and care should be taken that the needle does not pierce the same hole twice or the paper will begin to tear. The threads on the wrong side can be held in place with sellotape.

BELOW: *A collage of coloured handmade papers with added stitching, torn strips of spotted fabric and various threads.*

TOP RIGHT: *A paper incorporating a textured fabric and threads trapped within layers of pulp.*

BOTTOM RIGHT: *Textured threads sandwiched between several layers, give a raised grid of squares filled with simple stitchery.*

FAR RIGHT: *An example of paper with the added texture of lace. Some of the threads trapped in this piece have been pulled back into 'tear channels' in the top layer of the paper.*

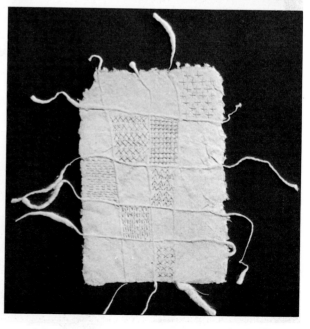

PRACTICAL HINTS

Mounting and framing

Framing gives embroidery its own space and helps to focus attention on the work. On a more practical level, it is a way of dealing with the raw ends. There are many different methods of achieving this and, with an art form that is constantly changing and exploring new ideas, care is needed to choose a solution which will complement the work and be sympathetic to a textile medium. The style of framing should also suit its setting.

Mounting should ideally be part of the whole concept and considered at the design stage, but this is not always possible with experimental work. Apart from the traditional picture frame, mounting may include soft, free-hanging surrounds which form an integral part of the embroidery; Perspex boxes — for very textured or raised work – and padded and embroidered fabric frames. Whichever method is chosen, make sure that the construction and the backing fabrics are strong enough to take the weight of the finished embroidery.

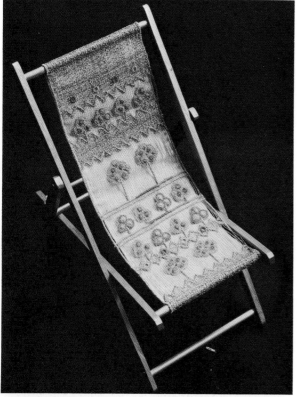

ABOVE: *This charming miniature deck chair is worked in machine embroidery on vanishing muslin. The finished embroidery is backed and mounted on a tiny wooden deck chair frame.*

TOP RIGHT: *Painted fabric is used for both the background and mount for this design based on a seed tray. The outline of the tray is made from thin felt covered with fabric and superimposed on the embroidery.*

Traditional frame with inner mount

The conventional picture frame with an inner cardboard mount can be used to great effect. The main problem with this type of frame is that the uneven texture of most embroidery makes it difficult for the card to lie flat against it. However, card does have the advantage of being easy to cut which means that unusual composite images less formal than the rectangle can be created. The mount may be cut to give the illusion of a doorway, window or arch extending the frame as part of the basic concept of the embroidery design. Similarly, the embroidery may be taken over the mount.

Mounting card comes in a range of colours, textures and weights. Choose a colour to complement the main tones of the work and make sure the card is substantial enough to hold the embroidery flat. Glass can dull the quality of threads and fibres, but it does protect the work from dust.

Free-hanging padded surround

This can be a form of fabric sculpture which may need firm support especially if it is to be hung, 'External quality' plywood is light and strong and is relatively easy to cut into irregular shapes.

Fabric frames

There are several different ways of making fabric frames. A simple fabric frame can be used on its own, or treated as another opportunity to add either embroidery, screen printing or raised work to the surround. The basic frame should be cut from hardboard or plywood, which is stronger than card — hardboard is recommended by conservators for supporting the back of embroidery as it is a neutral fibre and will not mark fabric over the years.

Lightly textured embroidery worked on evenly woven fabric can be cut on the straight grain and back stitched to another piece of fabric, leaving a border to act as a frame. Both fabrics can then be mounted onto a board using the lacing method.

A piece of embroidery laced to a board can be stitched onto another larger board covered with fabric. A curved needle will be needed to do this accurately. If the embroidery is heavy, screws or fixings will be needed to hold both pieces of board together for added support, and to prevent the backing fabric from being dragged down with the weight. On thicker mounts, metal or wooded strips can be added round the edges as a final finish.

Alternative suggestions for fabric mounts include using sympathetic types of embroidery together; for example, a border of log cabin patchwork, while appliqué works well with canvaswork.

Frames as a combined concept

Frames can be designed so that the embroidery and the frame are integral and dependent on each other. Clues to the ways in which embroidery could be extended in this way are often to be found in the original design ideas. For example a landscape could be extended by waved horizontal lines on the frame in a suitable technique.

Perspex boxes

Many people worry about highly textured or raised embroidery attracting dust and want some form of protection. If a simple style of frame is wanted, the work can be mounted on board, laced at the back, and covered with a perspex box. The disadvantages are that the boxes come in a limited range of ready-made sizes, and that reflections can detract from the embroidery.

Free hanging

The most obvious examples of frameless concepts are decorative quilts, banners and clothes, but many other abstract embroideries are also being produced that are designed to hang freely. An interlining is necessary for this type of hanging, and for banners, to prevent areas of embroidery or appliqué from pulling the background fabric out of shape.

The most straightforward way to hang them is on a smooth wooden pole. If the pole is to be a feature of the design, it can be threaded through fabric tabs attached to the top; alternatively a channel of fabric will hide the pole completely. The pole should be thick enough to carry the weight of the hanging without bending. Very heavy embroideries will need brackets screwed into the wall. Lightweight fabrics may need weighting at the bottom.

Public commissions

A panel hung in a public place needs extra considerations. Fire regulations will demand that some form of fireproofing is used. Slow burning fibres such as wool are recommended and should be used as much as possible. Always finish with a fire-retarding spray whether the embroidery is framed under glass or not. The panel will also have to be easily removeable for cleaning or repairing purposes, and extra precautions will be needed to ensure secure hanging to comply with safety standards.

ABOVE: *This panel, which depicts beds of tulips in a city park, is laced over board and surrounded by a narrow wooden frame which has been wrapped in threads. These echo the colours and design of the embroidery.*

Mounting and lacing To lace an embroidery over a wooden or cardboard block, begin by first establishing the exact area of the final panel. Using two 'L' shaped pieces of card, cover the raw edges keeping the straight grain if possible. Mark the corners with pins and tack out the shape. Cut a piece of hardboard, cardboard or softboard, a little smaller than tacked line. With embroidery right side down, place the card on top inside the tacked line. Secure with pins inserted into the edges of the card (**1**). Using a long length of strong thread, lace across working from the centre out and pulling thread tight (**2**). Complete second half (**3**). Repeat vertically, lacing under and over the horizontal threads working from the centre to the sides (**4**). Check that the front is still correct; adjust if necessary. Trim corner fabric to remove bulk. Complete the lacing (**5**). Cut out a piece of fabric to cover the back. Turn edges under and neatly stitch down (**6**).

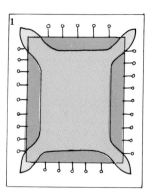
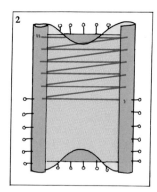
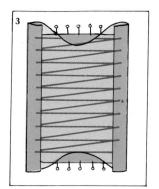
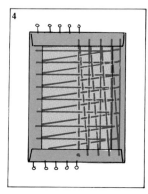
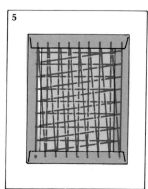
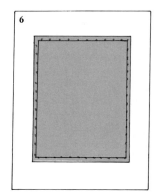
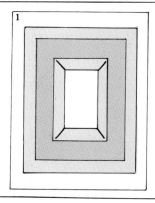
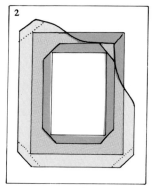
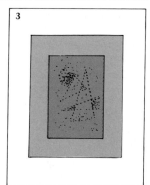
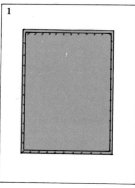

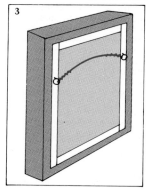

Fabric covered mount Cut out fabric to size of mount allowing half the frame width extra all round (**1**). Fold corners, crease and trim ½ in (12mm) outside foldline. Apply fabric adhesive to outer fabric. Fold over corners and press flat. Fold over long edges then short edges; press flat. Cut out the inside 'window' leaving half frame width all round. Snip into corners, apply adhesive; butt edges of fabric together (**2**) Frame the embroidery; stick or stitch in place (**3**).

Picture framing under glass, means that the embroidery should not be too deep. First stretch the embroidery over card as shown in Mounting and lacing (**1**). Decide on the colour and type of mount; cut out. Place the cleaned glass inside the frame, then the mount with the embroidery secured to it. Then cover with the frame back; (**2**). Secure with panel pins and gummed paper strip. Attach rings and cord for hanging (**3**).

Enlarging a design Enclose the design with a rectangle. Using letters and numbers to identify the lines, divide design into squares. Draw a diagonal line through design as above (**1**). Place design on a large piece of paper — bottom left corner and extend the diagonal line to height needed. Complete the rectangle and divide into same number of squares as original. Add letters and numbers (**2**). Draw in design free hand copying lines from smaller design (**3**).

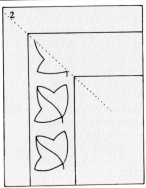 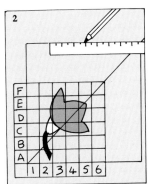 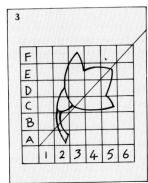 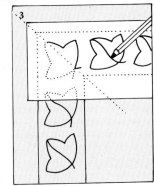

Corners To turn the corners of a design or border, place a small hand mirror diagonally across the design. Look at the reflected image and adjust the mirror to give a pleasant, even design (**1**). Mark the diagonal line (**2**). Trace the original border up to the line and reverse the tracing paper, as shown. Retrace the second half and repeat as needed (**3**). This gives a mitred corner effect.

 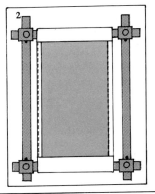 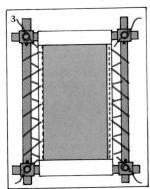

Dressing a frame Make ½in (12mm) turnings on top and bottom edges of fabric. Mark centres. Machine stitch 1in (2.5cm)-wide tape to other two edges. Mark centre of webbing on both rollers. With right sides together, attach fabric to webbing with small overcasting stitches. Work from middle out (**1**). Roll surplus fabric onto roller, slot in side pieces of frame and peg to hold fabric taut (**2**). Using strong thread, lace fabric to frame; knot ends around corners (**3**).

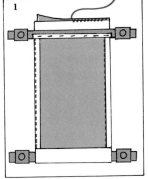

Damp-stretching Dampen the embroidery by spraying with water (**1**). Cover a board with several sheets of clean absorbent paper. Using lengths of string, pin out a rectangle to the finished size, (**2**). Dampen the paper. Place embroidery on top right sides aligning the edges with the string. Then working from the middle outwards and on opposite sides, gently stretch and pin to shape with drawing pings (**3**). Allow to dry naturally.

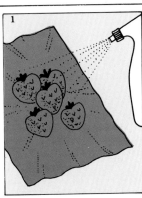 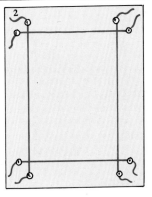 

WHERE TO LOOK

The Embroiderers' Guild, London
The Guild was founded in 1906 as an educational charity, and membership is open to anyone who is interested in embroidery. The Headquarters at Hampton Court Palace house a priceless collection of both historic and contemporary examples of the art of embroidery. There is also an extensive library for the use of members, as well as regular classes, workshops and seminars. There are over one hundred Affiliated Branches of the Guild throughout the United Kingdom which arrange their own programme of lectures and classes.

The Victoria and Albert Museum, London
The museum was originally opened in 1857 after being built with money derived from the Great Exhibition of 1851. The museum now contains one of the world's outstanding collections of fine and applied arts. Apart from this permanent collection there is also an ever-changing programme of exhibitions, lectures and seminars. The development of English embroidery from medieval times to the present day can be studied in the many galleries and also in the specialized Textile Study Room.

Museum of Costume, Bath
An extensive collection of costume from the late sixteenth century to the present day. It includes embroidered garments of 1580-1620, and of the eighteenth century, also whitework babies' clothes of the seventeenth and nineteenth centuries.

American Museum in Britain, Claverton Manor, Bath
A large collection of American quilts, both patchwork and appliqué, also hooked rag rugs and woven coverlets. The collection includes patchwork dating from 1770 up to the mid-nineteenth century. Many of the early pieces, which were worked by early settlers, show a great similarity in design to those made by quilters and rug makers in the North of England

Fitzwilliam Museum, Cambridge
One of Europe's major museums, the Fitzwilliam Museum houses collections devoted to the applied as well as the fine arts. The English embroideries include seventeenth century samplers, and stumpwork, and there are also examples of work from the Middle East, Greece and Turkey.

Gawthorpe Hall, near Burnley
The Hall houses the collection of the Hon. Rachel B. Kay Shuttleworth — a descendant of the owner. The comprehensive collection includes fine lace and embroideries from the seventeenth century to the present day. Many specialist courses are held at the Hall.

Hardwick Hall, near Chesterfield
An extensive collection of sixteenth and seventeenth century embroideries, including work attributed to Mary Queen of Scots and Elizabeth Shrewsbury, Bess of Hardwick. Also of interest are a set of appliqué hangings depicting 'The Virtues'.

Lady Lever Art Gallery, Port Sunlight Village, Merseyside
This notable collection includes large tapestries, many elaborate examples of English seventeenth century embroideries for caskets, mirror frames, and pictures. There are also some samplers and silk panels from the late eighteenth and early nineteenth century.

Burrell Collection, Glasgow
The art collection bequeathed by Sir William Burrell to Glasgow includes some fine examples of sixteenth and seventeenth century embroidery. The collection is now displayed in a new museum building opened in 1983.

Musée Art Decoratifs, Paris
The museum has a superb collection of particular interest to the designer and embroiderer.

Cooper-Hewitt Museum, New York
A museum of design with impressive collections of decorative art, furniture, glass, embroidery, woven and printed textiles and lace. It is designed as a reference centre for designers, researchers, scholars and students.

Local museums often have collections which they are unable to display but will show them if an appointment is made in advance. Information about exhibitions and courses are given in 'Crafts' magazine, published by the Crafts Advisory Council, London, and 'Embroidery', published by the Embroiderers' Guild, London.

Book list

Butler, Anne: *Encyclopaedia of Embroidery Stitches*, Batsford

Campbell-Harding, Valerie: *Strip Patchwork*, Batsford

Coleman, Anne: *The Creative Sewing Machine*, Batsford (paperback)

Dawson, Barbara: *Metal Thread Embroidery*, Batsford (paperback)

Dean, Beryl: *Embroidery in Religion and Ceremonial*, Batsford

Geddes, Elizabeth, and McNeill, Moyra: *Blackwork Embroidery*, Dover

Howard, Constance: *20th Century Embroidery*, Vols. 1, 2 and 3, Batsford

Kendrick, A.F.: *English Needlework*, A. & C. Black

Lancaster, John: *Lettering Techniques*, Batsford (paperback)

Lemon, Jane: *Embroidered Boxes*, Batsford (paperback)

McNeill, Moyra: *Pulled Thread*, Mills and Boon

Puls, Herta: *The Art of Cutwork and Appliqué*, Batsford

Pyman, Kit (editor): *Any Kind of Patchwork*, Search Press

Snook, Barbara: *Embroidery Stitches*, Batsford

Springall, Diana: *Canvas Embroidery*, Batsford

Thomas, Mary: *A Dictionary of Embroidery Stitches*, Hodder and Stoughton

Thomas, Mary: *Mary Thomas's Embroidery Book*, Hodder and Stoughton

Wardle, Patricia: *Guide to English Embroidery*, Victoria and Albert Museum (paperback)

Acetate sheet
A strong, smooth film produced in different colours. Useful for shadow work, decorating embroidery, and as a base on which to work needlepoint fillings. Available from suppliers of artist's materials.

Beeswax
A small, solid block of wax used for both strengthening and smoothing sewing thread. Used extensively in beadwork and metal thread work.

Bias
Any slanting or oblique line in relation to the warp and weft threads of a fabric. The true bias is formed when the selvedge is folded at a right angle across the fabric parallel to the weft and runs exactly at 45 degrees to the straight grain.

Binca canvas
A multiple-thread embroidery canvas woven with squares formed by the warp and weft threads. It is suitable for all kinds of coarse embroidery. It is not necessary to fill the ground completely.

Bodkin
A long blunt-edged needle with a large eye, used for threading tape, cord or elastic through a channel or casing.

Bolting cloth
Originally a fabric with a fine gauze or leno weave used for sifting flour, but a woollen variety was also used for children's samplers. It is now made from cotton, linen or synthetic fibres.

Bouclé
A novelty yarn, spun with random clusters of uneven loops along its length, usually with a hairy or tweedy texture.

Boxes
Panels embroidered at both sides of the yoke on the traditional rural smock, often featuring motifs of the wearer's home county and occupation.

Carded wool
Fleece from sheep, and other animals, that has been brushed over fine wires to remove impurities. The result is a well combed film of wool which is then ready for spinning.

Carpet thrums
Warp ends and waste thread left after weaving carpets, which is sold in mixed coloured bundles for domestic rug making, and canvaswork.

Chenille
Round, furry yarn, rather like a caterpillar in appearance. It can be made of wool, cotton or silk and, when stitched, gives a soft velvety pile. It is usually couched on to the ground fabric.

Chikan work
White embroidery from Lucknow (India) worked on sheer, white fabric using a variety of stitches including stem, double back stitch (shadow stitched), solid areas of French knots, buttonhole, satin and pulled fabric stitches.

Cordonnet
The foundation thread used to hold the working stitches of needlepoint lace.

Cordonnette
A thick thread or threads laid round the main outline of the design and worked over in close buttonhole stitch.

Damask
Reversible fabric, originally of silk, woven with an ornamental — often self-coloured design, usually a matt pattern on a satin weave background. The fibres used may also be cotton, viscose and synthetic, or a mixture of natural and synthetic.

Diaper pattern
Fabric woven with a small geometrical design. Sometimes applies to staggered rows which give the effect of diagonal lines, called bird's eye diaper. The same pattern is used in gold couching.

Dresden work
Type of drawn thread work on muslin made popular in the eighteenth century in Dresden, Hanover. It was made as a substitute for expensive bobbin lace.

Dressing
A stiffening agent of starch, gum, china clay or size found in new fabrics. Sometimes hides poor quality fabric but can also be an integral part of the fabric, as in glazed chintz.

Evenweave fabric
Linen, or other fibre woven with single, double or multiple threads, which has a clearly defined mesh on which embroidery can be worked by counting the threads. The warp and weft threads of true evenweave fabrics should be the same thickness, otherwise the resulting stitches will not be square.

Flower threads
Single stranded cotton embroidery threads sold in skeins, and produced in an excellent range of colours.

Glass tubes
Glass beads, larger than bugles, used in decorative bead work.

Grain
The line of the warp in woven textiles. To cut horizontally, along the weft, is called cutting across or against the grain.

Hessian
A strong, coarse fabric woven from hemp and jute in a fairly open weave. Used for ground fabrics, it is relatively inexpensive and good for experimentation and dyes well.

Kloster blocks
Blocks of geometrical satin stitches worked over an even number of threads to cover the cut edges in Hardanger embroidery.

Maquette
A small, preliminary model made as a trial piece prior to making the final work.

Mitre
The diagonal line formed at 45 degrees to the edges of fabric joined to form a 90 degree angle, or when two hems meet at a square corner. Makes a strong, neat corner.

Nap
Soft, downy raised surface given to some woven fabrics by a finishing process. If the raised nap looks a different shade from opposite angles, it may lie in one direction, as in a pile surface.

Oya edging
Traditionally embroidered by Turkish women to decorate their head squares. The colourful motifs, usually in the form of fruit and flowers are worked in the finest cotton, linen or silk thread using buttonhole stitch and tiny beads.

Passing
Metal threads, including pure gold and silver, made with a solid core. These threads are usually couched on to the surface of the fabric with decorative stitching.

Pearl purl (or bead purl)
Hollow metal threads made from convex shaped wire that look like a string of tiny beads. Used for outlining.

Picots
A series of small decorative loops, usually forming an edging on machine embroidery, and an integral part of cutwork and lacemaking.

Pintucks
A series of very narrow tucks stitched on the right side of the fabric and used as decoration.

Plate
A broad, flat metallic thread, usually gilt, with a very bright, shiny surface. Can be crimped to give texture.

Purl
Made up of finely drawn metallic wire coiled tightly round into a spring-like spiral. It is made in lengths of about 39in (1metre) which are then cut into lengths as needed. Purls are threaded on to a needle and stitched in place like beads.

Rocailles
Trade name for transparent beads used in embroidery. They are divided into three groups: round rocailles, or seed beads, are round with round holes; toscas are square rocailles with square holes but are rounded outside; charlottes are faceted on the outside.

Rolag
A roll of soft wool formed after the fleece has been teased and carded, ready for spinning.

Sateen
A strong, lightweight fabric with a satin weave running across it. It has a glossy sheen on one side only. It is relatively inexpensive and available in a good range of colours; it is usually made from cotton.

Seeding
Small embroidery stitches worked in a random, all-over way to fill an area, or worked gradually to soften an edge.

Scrim
Fine openweave canvas of a light brown colour, originally made from low-grade linen but may be cotton or a mixture of other fibres. Suitable for counted thread work, backgrounds and as a backing fabric.

Silk noile
Inexpensive silk fabric. The waste fibres which are too short for spun silk are carded and spun into coarser yarns, and woven into a dress-weight fabric.

Slate frame
A wooden frame consisting of two rollers with webbing attached and two side pieces with slots at the ends to take the rollers. The side pieces have a series of holes in which pegs or screws can be inserted and adjusted to give the right amount of tension to the fabric.

Slips
Traditionally, an embroidered motif showing a flower with stem and foliage and with a small piece of root attached. Ready worked slips can be cut out and applied separately to a ground fabric.

Slub
An unevenly spun yarn with alternating thick and thin areas randomly placed which, when woven, gives a characteristically knubbly texture to the finished fabric.

Soutache braid
A pliable, narrow plaited braid, similar to russia braid, used for appliquéd decoration such as outlining, interlacing patterns and initials.

Stiletto
A very sharp pointed tool used in embroidery for making eyelets in broderie anglaise, cutwork and eyelet embroidery. It may also be used in metal thread work for making holes in the ground fabric through which the ends of heavy threads are taken to the back.

Twill
Type of weave in which a diagonal line is produced in the fabric. In each line of weft a different series of warp threads is covered, though always in the same relation. Twill-woven fabrics are stronger than plain-woven fabrics.

Tambour work
Type of embroidery worked in a frame with a tambour hook. The designs are worked in continuous lines of chain stitch. It is often associated with whitework embroidery.

Vanishing muslin
Stiffened, treated muslin used as a backing or support for some hand and machine embroidery. The stitching is done through both layers and the surplus muslin vanishes when pressed with a warm iron.

Voiding
Part of the design where the unworked areas define the pattern and the background fabric shows through. The technique is, in effect, similar to stencilling.

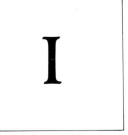

S

T

V

W

Z

ACKNOWLEDGEMENTS

The Embroiderers' Guild Collection: **p2** Claire Johnson, **p6** (left), **p6** Caroline Pitcher (right), **p28, 29** Jennifer Fox (left), **p39** Fiona Horcroft, **p47** Chrissie White, Verlie Reeve (right hand side), **p49** Isabel del Strother, **p52, 54, 55** K. Lesley Woodward, **p58** (top right), **p59, 60, 61, 62, 63, 65, 66, 68** (right hand side), **p70, 71, 77, 79, 83** (top left), **p90, 95, 96, p99** Jennifer Fox, **p106, 107, 108, 110** Lorna Weston (top), **p111, 113, 114, 115** (bottom), **p116** (right), **p126, 127, 131** Dorothy Walker, **p134-135, 136, 138, 139** Sue Rangeley, **p142, 143, 145, 146, 147, 148, 149, 176** Joanne Satchell, **p180** Vicky Lugg (top), **p180** Dorothy Walker (bottom).

Victoria and Albert Museum Collection: **p18, 82, 117, 122**; Dorset County Museum: **p71** (top left); Salisbury Cathedral-Sarum Group: **p116, 123**; Jeanette Durrant Collection: **p147** (bottom left); Herta Puls Collection: **p62, 86, 87, 91**; Sheila Miller Collection: **p67, 106, 115**.

Anthony Best: **p36** (top), **44**; Muriel Best: **p14, 34, 35** (left), **p38** (top), **p48** (bottom), **p50** (bottom), **p51** (bottom), **p58** (bottom), **p82** (right), **p83** (bottom), **p172, 173, 174, 175**; Jenny Blackburn: **p40** (top left), **p61**; Sylvia Bramley: **p129, p130** (right), **p132, 133**; Jenny Bullen: **p33, 47** (bottom left), **p66** (right), **p67** (bottom), **p93, 103, 105, 130** (bottom left), **p178** (bottom right); Valerie Campbell-Harding: **p101**; Hazel Chapman: **p130** (top left); Christine Cooper: **p77** (bottom), **p79** (right), **p94, 97, 100, 102** (right), **p154** (top left); Constance Howard: **p63** (top right); Vicky Lugg: **p15, 17, 18, 19, 30, 31, 36, 37, 38, 43, 44, 45, 46, 51** (right), **p55** (top left), **p76, 126** (top right), **p154** (bottom), **155, 156, 157**; Sheila Miller: **p51, 114** (left), **p123** (bottom left); Jean Mould: **p164, 165, 166, 167**; Daphne Nicholson: **p52, 53**; Maureen Pallister: **p40** (bottom), **p158, 159**; Herta Puls: **p88, 89**; Margaret Rivers: **p27, 40** (top right), **p48, 50** (top right and left), **p56, 160, 161, 162, 163, 29** (top); Dorothy Tucker: **p26, 35, 37** (top), **p69, 72, 73, 152, 168, 169, 170, 171, 178, 179, 181**; Marjorie Williams: **p42** (bottom); Mary Voules: **p41, 150, 151, 153**.